MERCEDES

· T · H · E ·

Enduring Legend

Text and photography by

NICKY WRIGHT

DEDICATION

To my wife Becky. Without her patience, understanding, typing, proofing, picture selections, and tending to our children this book would not have been possible.

Also to Phyllis and Conrad Mora of Pembroke Pines, Florida, and Dr. Philip Lutfy of Phoenix, Arizona, whose untiring help made this book possible.

ACKNOWLEDGEMENT

The author gratefully acknowledges the invaluable assistance provided by the following individuals and organizations throughout the preparation of this book:
Gary F. Lang; Andy and Barbara Englehardt; Lee McAlister; Conrad and Phyllis Mora; L. Philip Lutfy, MD; Bernhard P. Weitnann; Bill Claypool; Larry Nicklin; Dwayne Mackie; Mrs. George F. Carr; James Pike; Harry L. Snyder; Marty and Betty Wanielista; Gerry and Jean Connick; Mr. and Mrs. Paul Brissette/fabulous "Pink Palace"; Charles and Sharon Fischer; Bruce Everard; R. Arvin Grabill; Thom Barrett; Mary Jo Wrona/Coldwell Banker; Cathy Snyder; Roy and Barb Hathaway; Mercedes-Benz; Mercedes-Benz Club of America, Inc.; A&M, Detroit, Michigan; Pentax Cameras; Fuji Films. With special thanks to Autohaus of 500 N. Federal Hwy., Pompano Beach, FL 33062.

DESIGNED BY DICK RICHARDSON
EDITED BY JOHN PHILLIPS

2355
This edition published in 1991 by Tiger Books International PLC, London
© 1991 Coombe Books
Printed and bound in Hong Kong
ISBN 1 85501 133 6

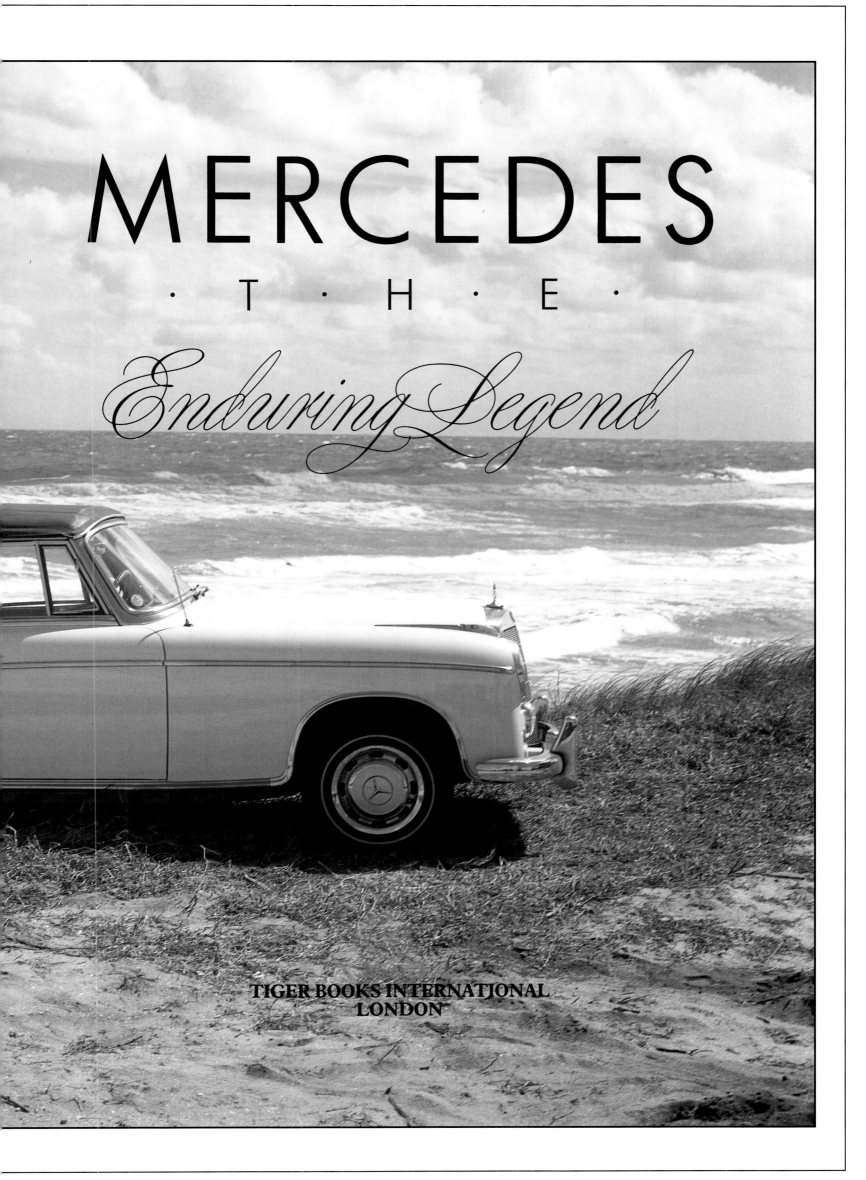

MERCEDES

·T·H·E·

Enduring Legend

TIGER BOOKS INTERNATIONAL
LONDON

INTRODUCTION

In 1885 there appeared an invention that would ultimately change the face of the earth for ever. It would be responsible for a revolution in lifestyle far more dramatic than any political upheaval over the centuries, past or present. This formidable creation would spawn new industries, stimulate mass employment, erode the class system, provide travel for those who had never traveled before and develop a new culture not appreciated by everybody, but understood by all. In 1885 Carl Benz invented the automobile.

Man's enthusiasm for his new toy not only brought tremendous benefits, but wrought terrible destruction as well. Millions of acres of virgin forest and green pasture gave way to concrete and clay and countless miles of black-top. The destruction of flora and fauna was one thing; the pollution of the air we breathe was another. Like with so many great ideas there has to be a penalty. Gasoline, besides fueling the automobile, has polluted our atmosphere, helped wreak havoc on the ozone layer and irretrievably damaged our ecological system to the point where another transportation revolution will have to take place if mankind is to survive the next two hundred years.

That is what the pundits tell us and there is little reason to disbelieve them. Nobody, however, can dispute the fact that the automobile has brought much pleasure to millions, be they Lords on high or honest-to-goodness garbage collectors. So much good has come in the automobile's wake that it is easy to forget and even to forgive its sins. And when Carl Benz invented the automobile he could see it only as a tool for the betterment of man's existence, since neither he nor anyone else knew that a Mr. Hyde lurked beneath the hood....

Carl Benz was 28 when he set up a small factory making supplies for the building industry in 1872, but only moderately successful, he decided, five years later, to change to manufacturing stationary two-stroke engines instead. Events moved quickly and the first gas-powered unit was ready for sale in 1879. By 1881 production was in full swing, the little engine selling reasonably well. Benz, however, was not satisfied; he wanted to develop it further – to drive a vehicle.

Benz & Co. Rheinische Gasmotoren-Fabrik was formed with several business partners in 1883 to develop and build engines under one roof (the first engines had been farmed out to another producer). This factory gave Benz better conditions in which to work on his ultimate goal: the self-propelled vehicle. He rejected the idea of a two-stroke engine as being too cumbersome and set to work on developing a four-stroke unit. In the autumn of 1885 the world's first motorcar – actually a tubular-framed tricycle - puttered out onto the street.

As with all great inventions, no one took much notice of Carl Benz' little gasoline-engined tricycle. Many, including his business partners, thought him a little touched in the head. After all, why bother with such nonsense when the stationary gas engine had become a runaway bestseller? And it had. So much so, in fact, that Benz & Co. had to purchase a sizeable plot of land on which to build a larger factory. Despite what people thought, Benz persevered with his three-wheeled car.

Despite the fact that this first vehicle had met with but little general interest, Emile Roger, Benz & Company's French agent, was so taken with the car when he visited the factory four years later, that he bought one himself. He became so enthusiastic that he persuaded the company to allow him to be sole agent in France for Benz automobiles.

Even Roger's enthusiasm did not communicate itself to Benz's partners, who still considered producing a car was a waste of time, and in 1890 they resigned. Their leaving was the best thing that could have happened, for the new board of directors enthused about the car and encouraged Benz to continue developing it.

Although the gas engine remained Benz & Company's mainstay, sales of the little three-wheeler continued to grow. Finally, in 1893, Benz introduced his first four-wheeled automobile, christened the "Victoria." This vehicle could be said to have been the world's first true automobile, although the Duryea Brothers of the United States may have disputed the claim, for they too introduced a four-wheeled motorcar that year. While there may be controversy over who produced the first four-wheeler, the evidence is irrefutable that Carl Benz ran the very first gasoline-engined car, even if it was only a tricycle.

By 1899 the Benz factory employed four hundred workers who busied themselves turning out the perennial stationary engine as well as a considerable number of cars. Nineteen hundred, the beginning of a new century, a new age, and Benz sold 600 cars to the moneyed classes who were much taken with this wondrous new toy. By now others had jumped on the bandwagon and Benz found himself surrounded by rivals from Britain, France, America as well as Germany itself. One rival, perhaps his main competitor and a man who would play a major part in motor history, was Gottlieb Daimler.

While Carl Benz was developing his four-stroke engine in his Mannheim factory, over in Bad Cannstatt, near Stuttgart, Gottlieb Daimler was designing his own four-stroke unit in a converted garden shed. Daimler had already designed a four-stroke engine, the Otto, for Deutzer Gasmotorenfabrik, the company he worked with for a decade. Following a difference of opinion between himself and the board of directors, however, Daimler left to go into business on his own, ably assisted by Wilhelm Maybach, who would eventually be the leading force behind the Maybach automobile. Between them they designed a lighter, more efficient four-stroke engine than the one they had built for Deutzer, and in 1885 they attached it to a bicycle for the purposes of testing. The following year the first Daimler automobile emerged from the shed at the bottom of the garden.

In a sense Daimler was more fortunate than Benz inasmuch as he wasn't hamstrung by a group of unsympathetic directors and was able to move much faster than his erstwhile rival. Soon Daimler and Maybach moved into their own factory, and in 1888 they signed an agreement with Panhard & Levassor that allowed the French company to build the Daimler engine under license. It is said this move marked the beginning of the French motor industry, which was to dominate the European car scene for many years to come. Following this lucrative deal, Maybach and Daimler formed Daimler Motoren-Gesellschaft in 1890. A few years later, in 1897, in order to keep up with the rising demand for its cars, the company purchased land for a huge factory at Unterturkheim, near Stuttgart, where production at the new facility began in 1904.

Daimler and Benz: two men following parallel courses in the evolution of the horseless carriage Though the events

Previous pages: the 1990 420 SEL, and (above) a 1956 300S coupé; two models that exude a feeling of quality and style.

surrounding their lives were remarkably similar, neither knew the other in the early years of the development of the automobile. In 1926, however, the two companies merged to form Daimler-Benz AG, based at Unterturkheim. By the mid-twenties, while the rest of the world was living the good life and dancing the Charleston, Germany's economy had, to all intents and purposes, collapsed. Inflation had reached such proportions that in the morning a postage stamp might cost one mark yet by the end of the day it would be several hundred. Considering the uncertain times and the fact that both companies had similar interests, it was apparent that a merger was essential to their survival in the grim economic climate of the day. The ensuing years have shown just how significant the move was to the development of motoring and the motor industry.

So far I haven't mentioned Mercedes. This name had absolutely nothing to do with either Benz or Daimler, yet it was to have a profound effect upon the motoring world in years to come, and was the name that would make other automakers apprehensive. Mercedes was the name of a pretty ten-year-old girl, the daughter of Emil Jellinek, the

Austrian General Consul in Nice. Jellinek was a motor enthusiast and loved to race whenever he got the chance. He particularly liked Daimler's cars and the story goes that he entered one in a race at Nice in 1899. For some reason he entered the car using the pseudonym "Herr Mercedes." His daughter's name must have brought him good luck, for he won the race and as a result Daimler sold several cars. From 1901 to the present day, the name Mercedes has graced some of the world's finest automobiles.

Gottlieb Daimler wasn't around to see the merger for he passed away in 1900. His company continued to be run by a board of directors and his son Paul, who succeeded Wilhelm Maybach as technical director in 1907. In 1921 the first supercharged Mercedes production car appeared and was very successful. So much so that when the legendary Ferdinand Porsche joined Daimler in 1923 he continued to develop the supercharger, culminating in the famous six-cylinder SS and SSK models. As for the merger itself, it was orchestrated by the brilliant Wilhelm Kissel, whose organizational abilities were second to none. Kissel, who had been with Daimler for several years, was named Chief Executive Officer of the combined companies and he set into motion a program of modernization and rationalization that would make Daimler-Benz AG the most efficient car company in Europe. Not everything he wanted to do was achieved, however,

15

for he met resistance to his proposals from both sides. Despite this, he was able to fulfill the greater part of his program.

Having survived the economic depression of the Twenties, Daimler-Benz entered the decade that followed in reasonable shape. This was due partly to Kissel's modernization plans, and also to the fact that Mercedes were expensive cars that sold only to the wealthy. Mercedes' racing prowess was another advantage for the marque; since the beginning of the century Daimler had been involved in racing, winning many prestigious races of the day, including the famous French Grand Prix. Most of Mercedes' racing successes in the early years can be attributed to Wilhelm Maybach, Paul Daimler and Ferdinand Porsche. Then, in 1929, Hans Nibel took over as Daimler's technical director and while he is most famous for the "Grosser Mercedes," a monstrous limousine powered by a 7.7-liter engine, the first swing axle Mercedes in 1931, and a brief adventure with a rear-engined model, Nibel constructed a 3.3-liter eight-cylinder racing car that developed 280 horsepower. This was the car that pushed Mercedes to the forefront of motor racing and marked the beginning of a period of dominance at the track for the Unterturkheim company. Unfortunately, Nibel died suddenly in 1934, but his work was carried on by his able assistants Max Sailer (who was the head man) Albert Hess, Fritz Nallinger and Max Wagner. Between them they piled racing success upon racing success, winning nine out of ten Grand Prix in 1936 with eight-cylinder cars that developed up to 600 horsepower. During 1937 victory came less easily to the mighty Mercedes even if they did win over half of the Grand Prix events. Sailer, Nallinger and Wagner redressed the balance in 1938 with a superb 3-liter twelve-cylinder racer that just about dominated everything on the track.

During the thirties Mercedes created some of the finest cars the world had seen; cars such as the Nurburg 500 and the Grosser Mercedes W07, a large and ornate limousine. From 1933 on, Mercedes became the official car builder for the top echelon of the Nazi Party. Of all the official automobiles, the Grosser W150 is perhaps the most memorable This car, like all the Grosser models, had a straight eight engine under the long hood. The engines were specially made for the Grosser series and all displaced a huge 467 cid (7,655 cc). Output has been estimated at 155 horsepower - I say estimated, because top-flight auto manufacturers didn't think it was anybody's concern how much power their engines developed. The 155 hp was the output without a supercharger; with it a heady 230 was realized.

Grosser production began with the W07 in 1930 and ended with the W150 in 1943. A total of 117 W07 models were built up to its end in 1938, when the W150 took over; only 88 of the latter being built between 1938 and 1943. In the interests of historical accuracy, there is a W150 circulating in the United States that is claimed to have been Hitler's personal car. This is quite untrue. Nevertheless, it does have quite a rich history, and Hitler once rode in it. This particular car was a gift from Hitler to Field Marshal Mannerheim of Finland. It was Hitler's way of saying how much he admired Finland for standing up to a belligerent Soviet Union. On 16 December the car was duly handed over to a nonplussed Mannerheim, who never liked Hitler anyway. But he didn't turn down the gift!

After the war, Mannerheim, who had been President of Finland since 1944, decided it might not be wise to be seen driving around in a vehicle so patently German and ordered it to be put away for a couple of years. In 1946

Mannerheim resigned as President and sold the Grosser in Sweden. After a couple of years in Stockholm and a period in the small town of Eskilstuna, the ex-Mannerheim W150 was used as a trade for American car parts, and on 18 June 1948 it was shipped to New York. By the time it reached the United States, the fabricated tale that it had belonged to Hitler was being circulated.

No one seems to know where this fine car is today. It is believed to have gone to ground somewhere in California, the last known buyer supposedly paying $500,000 for a car that had never actually belonged to Adolf Hitler.

Perhaps Daimler-Benz' most legendary model was the fabulous 540K. Introduced in 1936 as a successor to the 500K, the 540K was everything a sports car should be. Designed by Gustav Rohr, who succeeded Hans Nibel, the 540K was beautiful to look at, possessing a hint of romanticism not normally associated with German motor manufacturers, who tended to favor heavy, Teutonic lines.

Not only was the 540K beautiful, it was fast as well. Not by current standards perhaps, but certainly 0-60 in 15.5 seconds and a top speed of 120 mph was more than respectable for its day. The 540K's 5-liter (329.5 cid) straight-eight engine developed 115 bhp; if the engine was supercharged, horsepower climbed to 180.

Most of the 540's coach-built bodies came from Sindelfingen though a few were built by Erdmann & Rossi and there were the special order one-offs produced by individual custom shops. Even the British firm of Corsica, famous for its elaborate and unique designs (has anyone ever seen the wonderful Daimler Corsica sports car?), built an exciting Type SSK body in 1928. A few Hollywood types bought a handful of 540K models, paying something like $12,000 apiece. That was double the price of a V-16 Cadillac, one of America's most exclusive cars, but way below Duesenberg, which could cost up to $20,000.

As the world moved ever nearer to war, Daimler-Benz had passed the half-century mark. Its first fifty years had been eventful, and the company had come out of it with a string of racing successes and technologically brilliant cars to its credit. There was the rare Type 380, the SSK, the SSKL, the 500K and 540K. Then there was the sublime Grosser series, and the economy Type 170. Introduced in 1931, the Type 170 was Daimler-Benz' hedge against the Depression. It was also very advanced, with independent suspension all round (swing axles and coil springs at the rear).

With the outbreak of the Second World War Daimler-Benz production was given over to military projects, backed by Nazi funds as it had been since Hitler's rise to power. The consequences of the company's part in the Axis war effort was that Daimler-Benz factories and offices at Unterturkheim, Mannheim, Gaggenau and Sindelfingen were savagely bombed until there was almost nothing left. In short, Daimler-Benz had, to all intents and purposes, ceased to exist.

What you have just read is a brief record of what Mercedes achieved before war began. Daimler-Benz' first 53 years was filled with mechanical wizardry, genius and tumultuous events. The second period. from 1945 to 1990, shows no let-up in the dominance that has been Mercedes for over a century. Read on, study the photographs and you will see why, more than any other make, Mercedes has continually been the world's Number One automobile.

Facing page: the 280SL roadster, with its distinctive "dished" roof. As well as being a design feature, the shape of the removable roof added to rigidity.

The 170Va (these and previous pages), a 1936 design, helped put Mercedes back on its feet after the war. This model was built from May 1950 until April 1952.

CHAPTER ONE
THE LONG ROAD BACK

1945. What was left of Germany resembled a rubbish tip; people once proud were reduced to fighting over a scrap of bread. Whole streets were piles of rubble and dust; complete factories had disappeared, including Daimler-Benz. But Daimler-Benz was made of stern stuff. Surveying the destruction, the company's directors decided to make use of the few buildings still standing. Like a Phoenix from the ashes, Mercedes once again carried its three-pointed star proudly before it on the highways and byways of the world.

There was much to be done. While speedy rebuilding got under way, the factories – or what was left of them – kept themselves busy repairing and servicing pre-war models. Such was the speed of rebuilding that by June 1946 Daimler-Benz began producing commercial vehicles again. Within weeks of starting up commercial lines, the first post-war Mercedes Benz automobile left the factory at Unterturkheim. It was the successful 170V albeit unchanged from its pre-war days, but it was a start; after all, British and American factories were churning out warmed over pre-war models so why not Mercedes?

First shown at the 1936 Berlin Auto Show the 170V was a departure from the original first introduced in 1931. Whereas the earlier model had a box section chassis the 1936 170V sat on a tubular backbone frame, the same as the one used on Mercedes' rear engined 130H, 150H and 170H, all of which appeared between 1934 and 1935. Like all Mercedes the 170V was way ahead of its time. It came with all independent suspension (the famous – or infamous

SPECIFICATION
1952 TYPE 170V, Va/Vb

Engine: Four-cylinder. Bore and stroke: 75 x 100mm. 1767cc. Bhp: 45 (DIN) at 3600rpm. Compression ratio: 6.5:1. Manufacturing designation: W136. Built: May 1950 – April 1955. Number manufactured: 49,367.

– swing axle arrangement at the rear, which lasted into the sixties), a 1,700 cc four-cylinder, 38-hp engine with a top speed of only 62 mph and four-wheel hydraulic drum brakes. This was the car that started Mercedes on its post-war way in 1946, though the first models were variations on a theme; early production consisted of small delivery trucks, vans and police cars. The 170V lasted until May 1950 when it was given a slightly larger engine (1,767 cc) and became the 170Va. Horsepower went up to 45 and the ride was improved with the addition of softer springs and telescopic shock absorbers. Further improvements welcomed the 170Vb which replaced the 170Va in May 1952 but the improvements were mostly cosmetic, such as a smoother hoodline. A bigger windshield, wider track and a hypoid rear axle completed the picture.

Between 1946 and September 1953 a total of 49,367 170V, 170Va and Vb models were built. Bearing in mind the period, this was not inconsiderable. Not the most glamorous of cars perhaps, but good. solid transportation that could be relied upon when it was needed most. However, by 1949 much rebuilding had been accomplished and Mercedes added a second model: the 170S, in reality a development of the 170V but with a 7-inch longer body (which was based upon the pre-war Type 230).

Engine size of the 170S was the same as the 170Vb, at 107.5 cubic inches (1,767 cc). Horsepower was 52 and the car could canter along at 75 mph. The valves were set side by side and the detachable cylinder head was manufactured from light alloy. Improvements to handling and ride were accomplished with the use of a rigid X-shaped frame of oval tubular sections. This plus the all independent suspension, coupled with good weight

distribution, gave the 170S an outstanding ride, perhaps the best in its class at the time.

Model range of the 170S included a convertible, coupé and sedan and remained in production from 1949 to 1951: the sedan continued until 1953. There followed the 170Sb in January 1952 which lasted until August 1953. Changes included the removal of the gear shift lever from the floor to the steering column and the model also offered improved heating and a starter knob on the dashboard. Then came the last of the 170S series. Introduced in July of 1953, the new 170S-V was an amalgamation of the V and S models. The car had the 45 hp engine from the 170V, the Sb chassis, the S model's body and the front axle of the 170V. Then in February 1955. the final S-V left the factory and while it did not have a direct heir, there were many other Mercedes variations to choose from.

One model so far not mentioned is the diesel 170D. Daimler-Benz had a great deal of experience with diesel engines, more so than almost any other automobile manufacturer. After the war, the conquering Allies weren't too keen to let Mercedes begin production again, but the Americans, who occupied the zone in which three of Daimler-Benz' factories were, didn't worry unduly, and hence the company was able to start as soon as it was

Sporting butterscotch paintwork, this handsome 220A (these and previous pages) blends well with the desert landscape. The ohc 133.9 cid six (top left) looks cramped under the hood, but there's no shortage of chrome trim (top right).

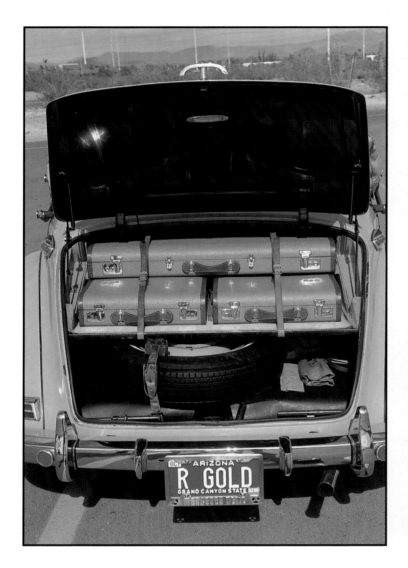

capable. However, when it came to diesel engine production, it was no, *niet* and *non* across the board. This was probably due to Mercedes' wartime production, when the company certainly built diesels for military vehicles of one sort or another.

Like many other major German companies, Daimler-Benz underwent careful scrutiny over its wartime past. Given a clean bill of health and after much Occupational red tape, the Allies finally acquiesced and gave permission for Daimler-Benz to build diesel engines. In May 1949 the first post-war diesel-powered Mercedes, a 170D, was introduced to the public.

Due to Daimler-Benz' first diesel foray with the 1936 230D, the new 103.5-cubic-inch four-cylinder engine (1,697 cc) was very durable and sold well over its six years of production as the 170D. Horsepower was 38 at 3,200 rpm and it delivered 32 miles to the gallon, an excellent reason for investing in such a car during those economically bleak years after the war. And Mercedes were not averse to economic thriftiness either; much of the diesel engine was shared with its gasoline driven equivalent. Commonalty of parts was all the rage with companies trying to find their feet after the conflict: surprising how parts-sharing became the "in thing" in the current world.

Motoring press reviews were good and the 170D sold 907 units in 1949, with a further 5,609 in 1950. The model was discontinued in May 1950 and succeeded by the 170Da. In April 1952 the 170Db continued the run until October 1953. These cars followed their gasoline-powered counterparts in tandem as did the 170DS and 170S-D, the latter pair using the 7-inch-longer body. The 170DS had a production run from January 1952 until August 1953; the S-D from July 1953 until September 1955. Interestingly , this

SPECIFICATION
1952 TYPE 220A

Engine: Six-cylinder. Bore and stroke: 80 x 72.8mm. 2195cc. Bhp: 80 (DIN) at 4600rpm. Compression ratio: 6.5:1. Manufacturing designation: W187. Built: April 1951 — August 1955. Number manufactured: 18,514.

was an eight month longer production run than its 170S-V counterpart, showing that the popularity of the diesel cars was quite considerable.

So far our tale has revolved around the Type 170 and its many and varied models. As the first Mercedes of the post-war period it has a historical significance. However, Daimler-Benz expanded its range in 1951 with the introduction at the Frankfurt Auto Show of the Type 220 and the ultra-luxurious 300 series. These were the first Mercedes to have all new post-war designs, both mechanically and bodily. The 1951/52 300 Cabriolet was particularly attractive.

The 1951 Model 220 four door sedan was quite a step up from the doughty 170. Good roadholding was matched by a degree of comfort normally the preserve of much larger cars: Cadillacs, Lincolns and Hooper-bodied Rolls limousines,

Custom-made, fitted suitcases (top left) were a nice option not found on other luxury cars. This particular 220A Cabriolet was bought in Zurich in 1975 by the current owner, who shipped it to Arizona in 1978.

SPECIFICATION
1955 TYPE 300S

Engine: Six-cylinder. Bore and stroke: 85 x 88mm. 2996cc. Bhp: 150 (DIN) at 5000rpm. Compression ratio: 7.8:1. Manufacturing designation: W188. Built: September 1951 — August 1958. Number manufactured: 560. 300SC built from September 1955 — April 1958 equalled 200 units.

for instance. What all 14¾ feet of the 220 possessed over the aforementioned was a refined and advanced suspension system; the others had a live rear axle and suspension too soft to be entirely safe.

Although the 220 had an all-new body, its basic design was still very much pre-war. Compare it to, say, a Jaguar of the period or almost any American car and the origin of the design will be obvious. At least the headlights were fared into the front fenders! Underneath the sheet-metal it was as we have already remarked, quite a different story. The chassis was a strengthened version of the 170's cruciform tubular oval unit and the power came from a SOHC in-line six-cylinder engine with a single carburetor. Unlike the clattery diesels – Mercedes hadn't found a way to remove the clatter – the six was very smooth and quiet running. A column shift lever took care of the fully synchronized four-speed transmission. As for the interior, the fit and finish of its appointments spelled luxury. In 1954 there came a major change: the 220 became the 220a and had an entirely new body, slab-sided and square in shape; the four-box design current at the time. The 133.9-cubic-inch (2,195 cc) six was given five additional horsepower, bringing it to 85. Length increased to 185.6 inches and the car's maximum speed was 93/95 mph. Although introduced in March 1954, the new 220 didn't go on sale until July of that year and remained in production until April 1956.

Meanwhile, there was the Model 300. As already noted, the 300 was introduced alongside the Model 220, at Frankfurt. If any Mercedes could be called beautiful at that time, it had to be the 300. It represented a return to the luxurious Mercedes of old; of uncompromising quality power and performance.

A 3-liter SOHC six cylinder engine was the 300's source of power. It had twin Solex downdraft carburetors, put out 115 hp at 4,600 rpm. and had a maximum speed of 100 mph, which was commendable considering the car's 4,000 lb weight. Perhaps the 14.7 mpg might have been improved, but the 300 was a luxury cruiser, and owners of luxury cruisers priced at nearly $7,000 don't worry too much about economy of operation.

Seven thousand dollars sounds a lot of money in 1951, and it was. Cadillacs were quite a bit less and certainly gave the buyer all the available options – except old-world craftsmanship. That the Mercedes had in abundance! Much effort had been expended on making the 300 not only luxurious – thoughts of the rich pickings to be obtained from the New World had a wonderful affect on incentive – but safe and roadworthy, too. All independent suspension (the usual swing axle arrangement at the rear) combined with coil springs and hydraulic shocks enhanced a ride made even better with

The early to mid fifties saw some of the finest Mercedes ever built. One such was the 300S series, shown on these and previous pages in coupé form. First exhibited in Paris in 1951, the 300S immediately found favor with the discriminating enthusiast. And it is easy to see why.

the use of hypoid bevel drive and dynamically balanced wheels. A worthy handling feature was the optional automatic torsion bar. If a switch located on the dash was pressed, the torsion bar "tightened up" thus allowing a firmer ride.

Another interesting feature adopted by other car makers later on, was the hydraulic steering damper. This worked by the use of a telescopic shock mounted between the frame and middle section of the three-piece steering linkage. It effectively cushioned all road shocks being transmitted to the steering wheel and was a great boon to driver safety.

Production of the 300 series was not what one might term prolific, in fact it was exactly the opposite. In not one year did unit production ever reach 3,000; the closest to that number was in 1952 when 2,921 units, including 262 convertibles, were built. In its last year only 46 cars were assembled. During its eleven-year existence, the 300 remained basically the same, with an increase in horsepower to 125 (DIN) in March 1954 with the 300b, and recirculating ball steering replacing the earlier worm and roller type. In September 1955 the 300b became the 300c, changes being entirely mechanical and consisting of two compound carburetors.

Then came the 300d in August 1957, the last of the line which carried on until March 1962. This was the only one to carry any bodily alteration, albeit a rather minor facelift, which included a squaring-off of the rear fender and trunk line, new chrome fender caps, larger headlight rims and new parking lights. Horsepower was raised to 160, a Bosch fuel-injection system replaced the carburetors, and automatic transmission was standard. Power steering was also available.

Until 1955 the 300 represented the most glamorous Mercedes available, the flagship of the fleet, as it were. It eschewed unnecessary change because, like Rolls-Royce, it did not need to change: it was, after all, a top people's car.

There was another 300: the 300S (the "S" stood for Super), which was displayed at the Paris salon in 1951. Unlike the regular 300 series which had four doors in sedan or convertible form, the 300S was designed for the discriminating sports enthusiast. The sort of person who might be seen in one of these elegant and swift automobiles might have been Prince Rainier, the Aga Khan or possibly Ava Gardner. The 300S was very exclusive, you see.

The output was 150 horsepower, the six-cylinder engine had three downdraft Solex carburetors and top speed was 110 mph. The interior had leather upholstery, and a choice of burl or straight-grain walnut was used for the dash and door cappings. Indicator lights were operated in a most curious way; the driver had to turn the horn ring left or right as was appropriate.

Production of the 300S ended in August 1955 and was immediately replaced by the 300SC, its production lasting

The majestic 300S measured 185 inches in length and 73.2 in width. Designed for the discriminating sports enthusiast, this was an exclusive model that harked back to the glory days of the big cars. A speedometer calibrated in kilometers (facing page top) identifies this coupé as a European edition. Turn signal, headlamp and parking light (facing page bottom) were logically arranged, but the six-cylinder ohc engine (top) wasn't the easiest to work on. Turn signal at rear (right) spoils the car's otherwise classic lines.

33

until 1958. This fine automobile had fuel injection, developed 175 hp, with its top speed now increased to 112 mph, and had a single pivot axle instead of the previous swing axle rear suspension.

By 1953 Daimler-Benz had recovered sufficiently from its wartime experiences to have become once again a force to be reckoned with in automobile manufacturing. Another area more worrying to those who remembered the pre-war years was Mercedes' return to motor sport. Already the Germans were making themselves felt with a relative newcomer to the field and that was Porsche. Mercedes, who dominated the race tracks in the late Thirties, could prove troublesome to Jaguar Ferrari and others. As before the war, Mercedes team manager would be Alfred Neubauer and the cars were created by technical director Fritz Nallinger and engineer Rudolf Uhlenhaut. One of those cars would eventually become one of the finest Mercedes ever built.

The 180 was launched early in 1953. It carried Mercedes' first truly post-war body and featured a break from its proven X-frame tubular platform. Instead Mercedes went to unitary construction and the 180 was the first model to do so. The basis for the new frame was high sectional steel side members to which the floor of the body was welded, which gave greater torsional rigidity and resistance to distortion. The front subframe was attached to the chassis on rubber blocks, and carried engine, transmission, steering and front wheel assembly. Although a first for Mercedes, it was not long before the majority of Daimler-Benz models were assembled this way. Different approaches to unitary construction were being experimented with by other car makers, and not twenty years would pass before the majority of cars would be built this way. As anybody who lives in a damp climate or where salt is used to clear roads of snow will tell you, unit construction can lend itself to the early demise of a car through rust. For once rust takes a hold the entire car will eventually succumb. Cars with chassis are not impervious to rust, but at least they can be saved to run another day.

So the chassis design was quite revolutionary at the time. Not so the engine, however, which was the 107.7-cubic-inch (1,767cc), 52-horsepower (DIN) four, borrowed from the Model 170S. Roomy, comfortable but not quite so economical (20.4 mpg), and possessing stubby lines in keeping with the then current trends, the 180 in its various forms (180a, 180b and 180c) stayed in production for nine years. Engine displacement was increased to 115.7 cubic inches (1,897 cc) from September 1957 (180a) with the resultant rise in horsepower to 65, then to 68 hp. With the 180b the 180c received new valve gearing and took the car into October 1962.

Like the 170, the 180 had a diesel-powered version called the 180D, introduced not long after the gasoline-engined one. Production started in October 1953 and continued until October 1962. The engine, which developed 40 hp (DIN) in the 180D and 180Db (1959) models, was identical to the unit used in the 170 series, and, like that series, both gasoline- and diesel-engined 180 models kept pace with each other. This is understandable considering the cars were identical apart

At 194.9 inches overall, the 1955 Mercedes 300 sedan presented an impressive profile (previous page). The solid mass of chrome and steel (right) is recognizably Teutonic.

The photograph facing page top shows it wasn't only American cars that had an abundance of chrome in the mid fifties. This particular model is a 300c, the first Mercedes to feature automatic transmission, though this feature only appeared towards the end of the run. Besides the three-pointed star, the radiator grille is a Mercedes trademark even to this day. A total of 1,432 300c sedans were built from September 1955 until June 1956, and 51 300c convertible sedans were constructed during the same period. The 300c was succeeded by the 300d from August 1957.

SPECIFICATION
1956 TYPE 300SL

Engine: Six-cylinder. Bore and stroke: 85 x 88mm. 2996cc. Bhp: 215 (DIN) at 5800rpm. Compression ratio: 8.55:1. Manufacturing designation: W198. Built: August 1954 — May 1957. Number manufactured: 1400.

from the engine and drive-train. Then in 1961 the Model 180Db became the 180Dc and was given a larger diesel engine, displacement now being 121 cubic inches (1,988 cc) and horsepower up to 48. The car took 36 seconds to reach 60 mph and top speed was only 15 mph more. Gas economy was better though: 29 mpg versus 22. Compared with the 180 model's 118,234 gasoline-engined cars, the diesel units numbered 152,983, which speaks well for the diesel engine's reliability. So confident were Mercedes of the diesel that several 180Ds were entered in the 1955 Mille Miglia, where they averaged over 60 mph over the 922-mile course and won their special class.

SL: the letters stand for "Sports Leicht" in German, "Sport Light" in English. These letters would achieve world renown within a short space of time with the numerals "300" in front of them. Tack the numbers and letters together, add the word "Gullwing" and you have perhaps the most desirable Mercedes model of the post-war years: the 300SL Gullwing. Today, one of these cars will fetch $750,000 in pristine condition, probably more.

It all started on the 2nd of May 1952, the day on which one of Europe's most prestigious races, the Mille Miglia, was being held. The Mille Miglia. 922 miles of tough road racing through Italy. All the top teams were present, including Mercedes. For the first time in thirteen years Mercedes had returned to the sport they had once dominated. It is not known whether it was because of their pre-war superiority that the Italians tried to have the Mercedes team expelled from the race, although their excuse was the gullwing doors of the Mercedes cars. The request for disqualification, however, was not upheld, and Mercedes ran a good race, driver Karl Kling piloting one of the cars into a well-deserved second place. A little over six weeks later Herman Lang and Fritz Reiss drove to first place in the 24 hour Le Mans marathon. The winning car was a Mercedes 300SL.

By 1949 Daimler-Benz felt confident enough to race again. Alfred Neubauer, the tough yet fatherly team-manager, found a pair of the 1939 3-liter racing cars at Unterturkheim and a couple more in a Berlin scrapyard. Racing was an expensive business even in 1949, so Neubauer had two cars made up from the four he had found.

Neubauer's great pre-war drivers were joined by a newcomer, an Argentinian called Juan Manuel Fangio. He, together with Kling and Lang, took the cars to the Argentine for the 1950 Buenos Aires Grand Prix and the Evita Peron Grand Prix. In both races Mercedes came second and third with pre-war cars competing against the very latest designs. These were the last races these cars ran.

New GP cars needed to be built, but there were snags. For one thing the then current GP rules had only two years

If ever a post-war car deserves to be recognized as a classic, then the Mercedes 300SL (previous pages and right) has to be the choice. The car looks right from every angle. Unique and stylish, the gullwing doors were carried over from the original racing version.

The interior of the 300SL (top) is as attractive as the exterior, the appointments including a set of matching luggage (left) fitted to the parcel tray, and a full complement of instruments. Turn signals and taillights (below left) are neatly integrated into the body. The rear view of the car (facing page top) is as pleasing as the front, although the doorline is very high, necessitated by the gullwing design. What little trunk space there is, is taken up by the spare. The 300SL sat on a 94.5-inch wheelbase and was 178 inches long overall. Top speed was over 145 mph.

SPECIFICATION
1957 TYPE 220S

Engine: Six – cylinder. Bore and stroke: 80 x 72.8mm. 2195cc. Bhp. 100 (DIN) at 4800rpm. Compression ratio: 7.6:1. Manufacturing designation: W180. Built: March 1956 – October 1959. Number manufactured: 58,708, of which 3249 were convertibles and coupes.

to run, and it would be pointless building a car which would take over a year to design and test if the rules were changed and that particular car's engine size and design were outlawed. Better to wait and see what the new formula was going to be. It was then that Chief Designer Nallinger and Research Head Uhlenhaut suggested that Mercedes concentrate on sports car racing, whose popularity was growing daily, not least in America. That first sports car racer arrived on the scene in 1952: the 300SL. The above discussions took part in 1950; by 1952 Daimler-Benz was putting the finishing touches to a 2.5-liter GP car, the size the new FIA Grand Prix formula would allow. Designated W196 and affectionately known as the Silver Arrows, Mercedes would repeat its pre-war GP racing dominance in the desperately few seasons the company allowed itself to compete. This book is not about Grand Prix racing, but the 300SL deserves particular mention for it was different; it became one of the finest production sports cars of all time.

It was designed around a multi-tubular frame that would give the car strength and be very light at the same time. Remember this car was going to be a production vehicle as well and had to be practical, necessitating easy entry and exit; to do this the space frame had to be extended higher to provide adequate beam strength between the wheels, and the high frame rails created a high, wide sill necessitating a radically new door design: the gullwing.

Three types of gullwing design were used on the competition 300SLs; the early cars had doors too small for comfort; then later the doors were larger and deeper. Open racers had doors hinged in the conventional manner.

The engine was a hotted up version of the six-cylinder unit employed in the Type 300 series. In fact much of the drive-train and suspension components came from the Type 300 albeit highly modified, of course. The space frame itself was constructed from chrome molybdenum tubes and the engine, transmission and rear axle were supported by three oval cross braces.

Although Mercedes did well at Mille Miglia on 2nd May,1952, they did not do well enough– if you call second and fourth overall not doing well enough, especially as this was the W194's first European race (W194 was the official D-B designation for the 300SL). This was but a small hiccup, though. Shortly after, Mercedes 300SLs came in first and second in the highly dangerous and exciting Mexican Road Race; first, second and third at Bern, then capped it with a one and three finish at Le Mans. Daimler-Benz was on target to dominate the racing scene.

After its crushing defeat of Jaguars and Ferraris in 1952

Made from 1956 to 1959, the elegant 220S has a 2195 cc six-cylinder engine developing 100 bhp at 4,800 rpm. Of the 58,705 examples built, just 3,429 were cabriolets (previous pages and right).

The three-pointed star (top) has long been a universal symbol of quality, and this is reflected in the fine condition of the original 220S interior shown above. Taillights (facing page) suggest an American influence. This car was driven from San Francisco to Atlanta, then on to Southern Florida, by owners Phyllis and Conrad Mora, which attests to the durability of Mercedes automobiles.

1958 MERCEDES 220S CABRIOLET

Daimler-Benz elected not to go racing in 1953; rather the company concentrated its efforts on Grand Prix racing the following year and developed an even stronger 300SL challenge for 1955. But the public was treated to the production 300SL in August 1954.

That the 300SL was a good car goes without saying. It was good because much of its racing experience was carried forward into the production vehicle, for example fuel injection, which was first used on the racing cars. This gave the six-cylinder sohc engine 215 horsepower (DIN) at 5,800 rpm. To facilitate a lower hood line the engine was inclined at a 50 degree angle.

Early bodies of this striking car were made of light aluminum, later a combination of steel and aluminum. It is said only 29 all aluminum bodies were produced and these are the most desirable of all as far as collectors are concerned. On the steel cars, hood, doors, trunk lid, rocker panels and belly pans were aluminum, so there was not a great deal of difference between the two. Suspension consisted of a swing axle at the rear, independent at the front, coil springs and tubular shock absorbers. Of course there were differences between the racing cars and the road-going SLs; a 45-gallon gas tank as compared to a 34.5-gallon one in the production car, and the latter had one spare tire instead of two. This was an advantage for the driver and his passenger taking a trip somewhere because it meant some trunk space. Another difference was a four-speed transmission in the production car instead of the five speed unit in the racer.

In magazine tests, 0-60 times were given as 8.8 seconds, which was good from the 182.7 cid (2,996 cc) engine hauling a weight of 2,849 lbs. Top speed was claimed to be 166 mph and judging by the car's tremendous performance, there is no reason to doubt this. As for the wonderful Gullwing doors, well, you had to be supple to negotiate the inordinately high sill and slide down into the seat. Talk about Hudson's step-down design! For the elderly, getting out of the car could present a problem.

Sired from a racing car with the thoroughbred of a racing car, the 300SL ranks alongside the world's greatest automobiles. From 1954 until the end of production in 1957, only 1,400 Gullwings were made. Not many more 300SL roadsters were made, either, for beginning production when the Gullwing finished in May 1957, the roadster was virtually the same except that it had no roof, apart from the convertible top, that is. And no roof meant no gullwing doors; instead the roadster had conventional ones, much to the relief of the less agile user.

Because convertibles need extra strengthening, the roadster's weight was 77 lbs more, but didn't affect the car's performance in the slightest. Actually it was better with 0-60 times of 8.2 seconds but top speed was about the same. Over the years there has been some controversy as to which is the better performing and handling car of the two. People fortunate enough to own both examples say the roadster wins hands down and this seems to be the opinion of testers as well.

In 1958 a hardtop was an option offered at extra cost, but in March 1961 four-wheel disc brakes were introduced as a regular production feature. The roadster lasted from

Previous pages and right: a fully restored 1958 220S painted in its original – and rare – two-tone livery. This is a fine example of classic Mercedes design. Whitewalls on this and other 220S are incorrect; narrow whitewalls didn't appear until 1962.

As can be seen on these pages, details of Dr. Philip Lutfy's 220S are first-rate. The view above shows off turn signal placement to best advantage. One of the few criticisms of Mercedes is the overly large steering wheel, an example of which is shown right. The chassis of this imposing car is unit frame and body, with an overall length of 183.9 inches (the sedan was 3.1 inches longer) on a 106.3-inch wheelbase (111 in. for the sedan).

SPECIFICATION
1959 TYPE 190SL

Engine: Four-cylinder. Bore and stroke: 85 x 83.6mm. 1897cc. Bhp: 105 (DIN) at 5700rpm. Compression ratio: 8.8:1. Manufacturing designation: W121. Built: January 1955 — February 1963. Number manufactured: 25,881.

Obviously encouraged by the 300SL's reception, Mercedes rolled out the smaller, less expensive, 190SL early in 1954. Production did not start until January 1955, however. Gullwing doors were not part of the package. As can be seen from the convertible examples shown on these and previous pages, the 190SL was a fleet and handsome car with an attractive interior to match.

The 190SL's four-cylinder ohc engine had a pair of dual downdraft carburetors, and a top speed of 106 mph. The wheelhub (above) is one of many attractive designs fielded by Mercedes. Strong bumper guard helps protect bodywork in the event of minor accidents. Overall length of 190SL is 166.1 inches on a 94.5-inch wheelbase.

1957 until 1963 during which time production was no more than 1,858 units.

The author has had no chance yet to drive the Gullwing but was fortunate enough to be able to sample the beautiful roadster belonging to Dr. Philip Lutfy of Phoenix Arizona. Dr. Lutfy collects Mercedes and has a couple of Gullwings. The 300SL Roadster is an experience to drive, its handling leaving little, if anything, to be desired and its four-speed manual transmission is quick, precise and a joy to use. Whirring through the warm Arizona night, flicking the stick, one, two, three, four and back, feel it bite, hear the engine's note change in perfect harmony. This is how motoring ought to be and thirty years have brought no real improvement. One cannot perfect perfection, and the 300SL Roadster is about as perfect a sports car as you could find anywhere.

Daimler-Benz didn't go racing in 1953, preferring to ready W196 GP car for the 1954 season. Then there was 1955 when it was going for the jugular with a much improved 300SL. After one or two shaky starts. the W196 roared to Grand Prix victory after Grand Prix victory. At the end of the year, 40-year-old Juan Fangio was crowned World Champion driver for 1954 and Mercedes was king of the racing road.

The much improved 300SL mentioned above was actually the 300SLR. It owed much to the successful GP cars, utilized a tubular space frame and was powered by the W196 2.5 liter (152 cid) straight-eight engine mated to a rear-mounted five-speed transaxle. Suspension was the traditional independent wishbone/low pivot swing axle arrangement. Bodywork was entirely different from the GP cars. Very low, very mean and bearing similarities to the production 300SL, the SLR made no bones about its intentions. This car was built to win. And win it did.

Alfred Neubauer had a good racing team; he had the cars, and he had the drivers. Of the new crop Neubauer enlisted a young Englishman by the name of Stirling Moss. Like a great many talented Britons, Moss would be remembered by colleagues as being fun to be with and charismatic to a fault. Everyone who knows people like that has stories to tell about them.

One concerns his memorable race in the 1955 Mille Miglia. Moss had asked well-known motoring author Denis Jenkinson – he with a Duesenberg engine in his garden shed – to navigate the nearly 1,000 mile course for him. Happy to oblige, Jenks, as he is known to his friends, plotted the course and studied the map until he knew it by heart. On the day of the race, with Jenks sitting beside him in the awesome 300SLR Moss didn't take long to realize that his colleague's navigating was so good that he would be able to take risks he wouldn't dream of with others. Therefore whenever a hill approached Moss drove at it at 170 mph and beyond, leapt the crest and "flew" for 50 yards or more. Although he couldn't see beyond the hilltop, he knew it had to be straight because Jenks said it was.

Moss drove that race like a man possessed, he and machine as one. He took calculated risks, stood on the accelerator for the entire race and passed everything in sight. The car became so hot that Jenkinson actually burned himself on the gearbox and lost his glasses in the slipstream in the process. Moss won the 1954 Mille Miglia in 10 hours, 7 minutes and 40 seconds, the fastest over-the-road speed ever attained.

Two years later the Mille Miglia was no more, banned because of the high loss of life. But those were the days when motor racing was truly an adventure, practiced by men of verve and great skill; when fun and danger drove together in great machines like the 300SLR.

CHAPTER TWO
WORLD CLASS FROM A WORLD LEADER

Just as the rest of the motoring world feared, Daimler-Benz had climbed back from the abyss and were conquering the best in international and European competition. Not only that but the production cars such as the race-proven 300SL, the 300 series and the 220 were recognized as being far more advanced than almost anything else on the road during the mid-fifties.

Perhaps realizing the 300SL would not be a runaway best seller – at a price of $11,500 it was hardly likely to cause a stampede into the showrooms – D-B announced a pint-sized, half-priced brother to the 300SL. Shown in 1954 and put into production from January 1955, the 190SL looked like an undernourished 300SL. Perhaps an unfair comparison, especially since the 190, once regarded as an ugly duckling, is a beautiful car. Today it has become highly collectible, and with good reason.

Using a modified, self-supporting unit body/chassis adopted from the 180 sedan, with a removable front sub-frame assembly to carry the engine, transmission and axle, the 190SL was subject to a few technical delays that had to be ironed out. This was fortuitous in a way because it meant D-B was able to adapt its famous swing axle suspension to the rear.

The engine for the 190SL was newsworthy because it was the first overhead cam four-cylinder unit ever used by

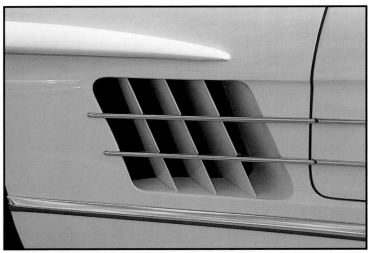

SPECIFICATION
1963 TYPE 300SL

Engine: Six-cylinder. Bore and stroke: 85 x 88mm. 2996cc. Bhp: 215 (DIN) at 5800rpm. Compression ratio: 8.5:1. Manufacturing designation: W198. Built: May 1957 – February 1963. Number manufactured: 1858

The 300SL is one of a number of cars fine owned by Mercedes collector Dr. Lutfy (he owns the 300SL Gullwing as well). The 300SL Roadster is considered by many knowledgeable enthusiasts to be a better road car than the gullwing coupé. As can be seen, the car has conventional doors, thus making entry and egress easier. Detail finish is exemplary if door handles and window winders (top) are anything to go by.

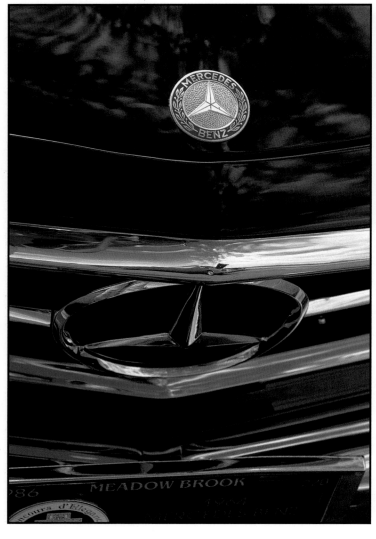

SPECIFICATION
1964 TYPE 230SL

Engine: Six-cylinder. Bore and stroke: 82 x 72.8mm. 2195cc. Bhp: 150 (DIN) at 5500rpm. Compression ratio: 9.3:1. Manufacturing designation: W113. Built: March 1963 -January 1967. Number manufactured: 19,831.

Successor to the 190SL was the 230SL, which first appeared in 1963. Although the grille was similar to that on the 300 and 190SL models, everything else, from interior to taillights, was different.

D-B. Designated M121, this engine shared the Type 300SL's ohc six-cylinder bore of 3.35 inches. Its stroke was quite a bit different, however: 3.29 versus the 300SL's 3.46. The engine's displacement was 115.7 cubic inches (1,897 cc) and horsepower was 105 (DIN). Of course, with its much smaller engine than its bigger brother, the 190SL couldn't hope to keep up in a traffic-light grand prix, but a top speed of 106 mph was still quite impressive.

Where the 190SL really scored was in production. Between 1955 and February 1963, when the last one came off the line, 25, 881 units had been built, costing $3,998 each in 1955, rising to a little over $5,000 by the end of the run. This was over a thousand more than a 327-cubic-inch 1962 Corvette, though comparisons might be a little unfair. The American car was strictly brute force and ignorance; the 190SL a refined little jewel.

Back in the racing saddle with a vengeance, Mercedes were dominating road and track events by 1955. Mercedes had entered a team to compete in the great 24-hour Le Mans race on 11 June, 1955, Stirling Moss, Juan Fangio, Herman Kling, Andre Simon and Pierre Levegh being the drivers. A few hours into the race and the great silver 300SLRs were pouring it on, looking for yet another victory. Levegh was attempting to pull away from two other cars and the three racers came down the straight, past the packed grandstand at speeds of 125 mph and increasing all the while. Then tragedy struck. Pierre Levegh's Mercedes collided with one of the two cars beside him. The great silver car flew into the air and smashed, blazing, into the grandstand. The white-hot engine tore a bloody hole through the spectators while pieces of jagged, burning metal caused indescribable damage to frail bodies. It was all over, save for the moans of the wounded and the dying. Eighty people died and 100 others were injured, some seriously, in this the worst motoring accident in the long history of the sport.

With the horror of the tragedy being enacted in the crumpled stands, the race was surprisingly allowed to continue. Eight hours after the accident, Moss/Fangio led the field in their SLR while Kling/Simon were placed third. Then a message from Fritz Nallinger in Unterturkheim was delivered to team manager Neubauer ordering the entire Mercedes team to withdraw, as a sign of respect for those who had died, and their families. The pit crew signalled the SLRs to come in, which of course they did. But the race still went on.

"In spite of the horror of the situation," said the course director, "I did not judge that the race should be interrupted. Even when tragedy happens, the sport should be guided by its own law." Understandably, the course director was not the most popular man in France, after that. Few, if any, agreed with his decision or explanation, dismissing the man as cruel and callous. Following Le Mans, Mercedes said it would not race at any track that did not have adequate safety provisions. Four GP races were cancelled due to the tragedy; Mercedes won the three remaining events. At the season's end Daimler-Benz announced its withdrawal from competition; in two years Mercedes had come from nowhere to win nine Grand Prix out of thirteen raced; 42 cars were entered and 27 finished.

From 1956 until the late Eighties, Mercedes concentrated

Proportions can be deceptive: one would think the 230SL to be smaller than its predecessor. In fact its wheelbase length of 94.5 inches is the same, but overall it was two inches longer, 168.6 vs. 166.1 inches.

SPECIFICATION
1967 TYPE 600

Engine: V8. Bore and stroke: 103 x 95mm. 6332cc. Bhp: 250 (DIN) at 4000rpm. Compression ratio: 8.8:1. Manufacturing designation: W100. Built: August 1963 – June 1981. Number manufactured: Limousine 2190; Pullman 487.

all its talents on superior sedans and road going production sports cars. Announced at the 1956 Frankfurt Auto Show were three new models: the 190 sedan, the 219 and the Model 220S. Sharing the 180's body, the 190 was powered by the four-cylinder ohc unit first used in the 190SL, with bore, stroke and displacement the same but the engine detuned to 75 hp (DIN). Like the other two models, the 190 had a unit body and frame and Mercedes' tried and true independent front, swing axle rear suspension. The 190 stayed in production until 1965 and in 1959 horsepower was upped to 80 and the 7.5:1 compression ratio increased to 8.5:1. In 1961 the 190 was given a new body - slab sides, a crease running the length of the car and little fins which were very slightly canted. Compression was up to 8.7:1 and the car grew nearly 10 inches, to 186.5 inches. This finned Mercedes became famous without meaning to. It was popular as a taxi in Central Europe, the Middle East and certain South American countries, but its real claim to fame came as the Beirut Special; remember those news bulletins from Beirut, Lebanon, over the past fifteen or so years? About the only car one would see on the rubble-strewn streets was the finned Mercedes 190, perhaps the occasional 220SE or 300, all with fins, of course.

Another 180 clone was the Model 219 sedan. The wheelbase was stretched from 104.3 inches to 108.3 and the overall length was 7 inches more, at 184.3. As production and tooling costs rose so did increased rationalisation at D-B. Looking for an engine for the 219, the engineers opted for the faithful six-cylinder overhead camshaft unit once used in the former 220 sedan. An interesting, if unreliable, option offered was the curious Hydrak transmission made by Fichtel & Sachs. It was a sort of semi automatic, similar to the one used on the radical Citroën DS19. There was no clutch; the driver moved the transmission lever to the desired gear and it was automatically selected. Unfortunately there were a lot of burned-out automatic clutches, so the system did not enjoy great popularity.

The 220 (1956 – 1959) and the 220S that followed in 1959, both had the M180 six-cylinder ohc engine as used in the 219. Output was more: 100 hp in 1956, 106 in 1957. In May an attractive convertible appeared, and a hardtop coupé rounded out the series in 1957. Apart from the fact it was a refined, well-built car, there was little to distinguish it from many others, such as the cars already described.

Diesels continued to play an increasingly popular role; of the 190 series, the diesel, which was introduced two years later, in 1958 outsold the gasoline version by quite a wide margin (from 1961 to 1965, the diesel sold 95,091 more cars). The diesel engine used in the 190D was all-new. It had a shorter stroke and an overhead camshaft in place of the previous pushrod engine, and displaced

A carriage fit for kings, the Mercedes 600 – or Grosser Mercedes as it was commonly called – was sumptuous beyond compare. The model shown is the 218-inch limousine, but there was also a Pullman version that stretched to 246 inches, making it the longest production car in the world.

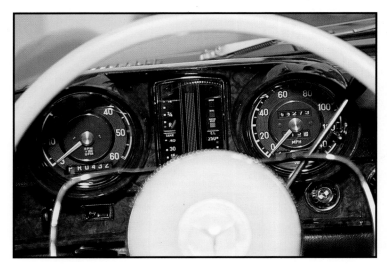

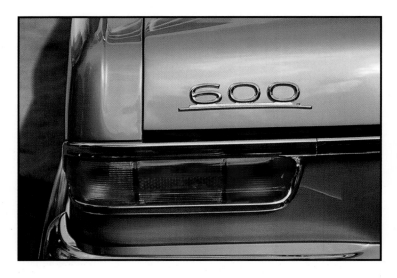

115.7 cubic inches. Horsepower was 50 (DIN) and the engine had a Bosch fuel injection pump, unlike the gasoline engine which relied on carburetors

One of Mercedes' most beautiful models was the stunning 220SE. This was in production from 1959 to 1965 and featured a 133.9-cubic-inch (2,195 cc), overhead camshaft six-cylinder engine rated at 120 hp (DIN). It wasn't the car's engine that attracted glowing praise from critics and public alike, however, but the two-door hardtop coupé and convertible that really caught the eye. Almost 192 inches long, the 220SE shared much with its sedan counterpart the 220 (1959-1965). Same engine, same suspension, same wheelbase. What made the difference, the silk purse out of a sow's ear, was from the doors back. On the sedan the rear was squarish, topped by the fins that really did not suit. The nameless designer – D-B does not appear to divulge its stylists' names – responsible for the SE, removed the silly appendages, rounding off the rear fenders as he did so. And the difference was as the difference between chalk and cheese. How a small alteration would turn a forgettable style (unless you happened to watch all the newsreels from Beirut) into a memorable one.

It cost $8,895 in America but was worth the price. Real leather upholstery, a four-speed automatic transmission, a dual braking system – if one cut out, the other cut in – all were included in the price, culminating in a fine car, beautifully styled and one of the top Mercedes of the post-war era.

Whitewall tires and more chrome were highlights of the new 300SE sedan. Besides these minor differences, the 300 shared its finny body with the 220 series. Air suspension and four-wheel disc brakes were standard on this 1961 car which stayed in production until 1967, although only some 9,000 were built in that period.

The horsepower of this well-appointed sedan was 160 (DIN), but gas consumption was as bad as the big block Americana, at 12 mpg. A 300SE convertible and coupé, both identical to the 220SE and just as desirable, were added in March 1962, the engine being a six-cylinder ohc rated at 182.8 cid (2,996 cc) and developing 160 hp; top speed was 112 mph. Later this same light-alloy engine was raised to 170 hp and the speed went to 124 mph. By now the car had become the 300SEL, the wheelbase had grown 4 inches to 112.2 and the overall length had also gone up 4 inches to 196.9 inches – what Detroit would have called an "intermediate" in those days.

Remember the W150 Grosser? A great and classic car built to the most exacting standards It only seemed fitting that a new Grosser be created for top. top folk such as Kings, Queens, Presidents and Premiers. With a return to an eight-cylinder power unit, if possible

The Frankfurt Auto Show has always been D-B's favorite launching ground for new models. In 1963 the first post-war Grosser the new Model 600 was unveiled. There were two versions: the enormous 5/6 passenger limousine or the gargantuan 7/8 passenger Pullman. Wheelbase and overall length of the limousine was 126 and 218 inches respectively. The Pullman had a mammoth 153.5 inch wheelbase and the overall length stretched to 246 inches. Or twenty feet six inches. We are told that American cars were big, but the 1963 Grosser 600 beat Cadillac's longest production car, the Fleetwood 75 limousine, by almost 3 inches!

Of course the really big news was the V-8. A first for Mercedes, this 6.3 liter (386.3 cid) unit had an overhead camshaft, one for each bank, Bosch fuel injection and developed 250 hp (DIN). Considering the limousine's 5,434

Nothing was too good for the 600 (these pages) – it boasted every available feature that could be had on a car, including air suspension, shock absorber adjustment, disc brakes, central locking, and air conditioning. Instruments were set in a wooden dash and all doors and windows were framed in wood. Headlights, turn signals and parking lights correspond to American laws – Europeans had halogen units set behind glass bubble. Three-pointed star reflects the elegance of this superb car.

SPECIFICATION
1967 TYPE 280SE

Engine: Six-cylinder. Bore and stroke: 86.5 x 78.8mm. 2778cc. Bhp: 160 (DIN) at 5500rpm. Compression ratio: 7.8:1. Manufacturing designation: W108. Built: November 1967 — May 1971. Number of coupes and convertibles manufactured: 5187.

lbs weight, the engine delivered enough power to rattle the big car up to 127 mph and do 0-60 in under 10 seconds Miserly with the gas the 600 most definitely was not. Between 9 and 10 mpg if one were lucky.

An incredible hydraulic system powered virtually everything in the car; from seats to trunk-lid, even to the car's doors. A slight push on any door would trigger a hydraulic ram that proceeded to close it quietly and effortlessly. Options such as a central divider window were also powered as was the sun-roof the latter operable by either front- or rear-seat occupants. The ride was not cloud nine soft like a 1958 Buick; it was solid, perhaps a little on the hard side. Even though the car had power steering and only 3.3 turns lock to lock, it was still an effort to turn the wheel. But the richly appointed interior, replete with leather upholstery, real wood and exemplary craftsmanship and finish, tended to make these criticisms so minor as to be forgotten.

Eighteen years after its launch this car of kings finally was no more; perhaps it had become an anachronism. Only 2,190 of the model 600 limousines and 487 Pullmans were built between 1963 and 1981 – 2,677, that was all. A truly great car that could take its place besides its illustrious ancestors with pride.

Which brings us back to the 300 series, specifically the model 300SEL. This was the second Mercedes model, and the first sedan, to adopt V-8 power. Specifications for the engine were identical to those of the 600, launched five years earlier. Obviously in a car weighing 1,606 lbs less and giving away almost two feet in length, the 300SEL should have decent acceleration. It did: zero to 60 flew up in 6.5 seconds and its maximum speed was recorded at 137 mph. This was American musclecar stuff, but no one likened the 300SEL to a musclecar. It was too well finished and refined to be considered in that league.

As the 6.3 neared the end of its run, there arrived on the scene in May 1971 the 300SEL 4.5. This smaller engine was the progenitor of a series of V-8 models that continued into the Eighties There were no more 6.3 V-8 models after 1972, and with only 6,526 built over five years, it is quite a collector car today. I owned one of these cars several years ago and can back up to the rave reviews the SEL garnered for itself. It had quality, exhilarating acceleration and comfort. The only fault was its somewhat unpredictable road manners. Unless one was careful one could easily lose the rear due to its swing axle suspension. Depending on the camber of the road surface and the car's driving position, the rear wheels could tuck in on themselves. It did not happen often but it was alarming if this occurred without warning. When the new S-series arrived in 1972 this problem was solved with a new suspension system.

Lasting only one year the Mercedes 300SEL 4.5 could

As different from the 600 as chalk is from cheese, the 280SE coupé (these and previous pages) was one of the most attractive Mercedes ever built. Sitting on a 108.3-inch wheelbase, the designers spread its proportions well over its 192.9-inch total length. The car's 169.5 cid six-cylinder ohc engine developed 160 bhp (DIN) and offered a maximum speed of almost 120 mph.

SPECIFICATION
1969 TYPE 280SL

Engine: Six-cylinder. Bore and stroke: 86.5 x 78.8mm. 2778cc. Bhp: 170 (DIN) at 5750rpm. Compression ratio: 9.5:1. Manufacturing designation: W113. Built: November 1967 – March 1971. Number manufactured: 23,885.

be regarded as a transitional model between the old and the new, the new being the shortly to be introduced S-series. Like all Mercedes the 4.5 was a good car that was much favored by those who couldn't afford a Grosser 600 but liked to be chauffeur driven. Horsepower from the 275.8 cubic inch engine was 225 (DIN) and the car would drive happily to 127 mph. An interesting suspension modification was the inclusion of anti-sway bars, which began appearing on a number of the pre-S class Mercedes from 1969 onward. Contemporary road tests show this particular model as being an excellent performer with handling to match.

Before the 4.5 there was the 3.5. Introduced as the Model 300SEL 3.5 at the 1969 Frankfurt Auto Show, the car employed the same body as the earlier six cylinder 300SEL. This 213-cubic-inch unit developed 200 hp (DIN) and had the same turn of speed as the earlier-discussed 4.5. It, like all Mercedes, was very advanced and came with self-levelling air suspension and many convenience features found on the 6.5-liter model. The 300SEL lasted until 1972, and during its run 9,483 units were made.

During the period 1967 to 1972 the Mercedes model range proliferated at an enormous pace for there was something like eighteen different models sharing four wheelbases. Most were sedans sharing either the 108- or 112-inch wheelbase, but two models were entirely different, with wheelbases of 111 and 96.9 inches respectively. Both were V-8 powered and both were sports cars. The Model 350SL and 350SLC were direct descendants of the 230SL, launched in 1963 as a successor to the 190SL.

First shown to the world at the March 1963 Geneva Auto Show, the 230SL was well received by the public. It didn't look anything like its predecessor, the designers shunning the 190SL's rounded curves for a squarer more sedate look. Power came from the old warhorse overhead cam six cylinder engine, Mercedes' backbone in one form or another since its inception, in 1951. By the time this loyal unit reached the 230's engine bay it had been developed and refined to a point that it could hardly be taken any further.

For use in the 230SL the engineers raised displacement to 140.7 cubic inches (2,306 cc), replaced the two-plunger fuel-injector pump with a six-plunger one, and increased the bore from 3.16 to 3 23 (80 mm to 82 mm), thereby raising the horsepower to 150 (DIN) at 5500 rpm. This gave the 230SL a reasonable maximum of around 125 mph which was at least 20 mph faster than the 190SL. Acceleration from 0 to 60 though, was a bit on the slow side at 11 seconds; any self-respecting Jaguar E-Type would have left it standing at the crossroads.

Between 1963 and 1967, 19,831 Mercedes 230SL models were built; soon the little sports car with the concave roof

First came the 230SL in 1963, then the all-too-brief 250SL (it lasted thirteen months, from December 1966 until January 1968), which was immediately followed by the 280SL coupé/roadster shown on these and previous pages.

This car can be referred to as either coupé, roadster, or coupé/roadster due to the removable hardtop roof which was of unique concave design (above and facing page). Taillights were the same throughout the series. The wheels (above) are not original to this model – they come from a later 450SL roadster.

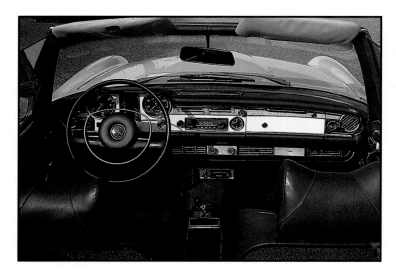

*Previous pages and right: another 280SL coupé/roadster.
This car has been a daily driver since it was purchased new
in Germany. The owners toured Europe for two months
before returning to America. In 1971 they sold the car to the
present owners, Mr. & Mrs. George Carr. As can be seen, this
280SL is in good shape considering it has never been
worked on. Wheel (above) is correct for this model.*

SPECIFICATION
1979 TYPE 300D

Engine: Five-cylinder. Bore and stroke: 91 x 92.4mm. 3055cc. Bhp: 80 (DIN) at 4000rpm. Compression ratio: 21:1. Manufacturing designation: W123. Built: July 1975/February 1976 -. Number manufactured: N/A.

Mercedes have always been at the forefront of diesel engine technology and the five-cylinder, 80 bhp unit powering the 300D (these and previous pages) is no exception. With a length of 186 inches on a 110-inch wheelbase, this particular body was shared with eight other models and was first shown at Geneva in 1976.

became a familiar sight in and around Beverly Hills. Nineteen months after the launch of the 230SL D-B introduced a new six-cylinder engine. Cost limitations didn't allow for a totally new power plant so there was some sharing with the old six (M127), such as the cylinder centers with the cylinders joined together in pairs. Also new were molybdenum piston rings instead of the previously used chrome. Molybdenum withstood far higher operating temperatures.

The new engine, designated M129, had an aluminum cylinder head, sodium-cooled exhaust valves with stellite faces. Valve seat inserts were resistant to wear and the longer stroke unit had a seven-main-bearing crankshaft instead of the four-main-bearing one. These and many other improvements resulted in an altogether better engine in every way. Finally, displacement was increased to 152.3 cubic inches compared to the M127's 140.3, developing 150 horsepower (DIN) at 5,500 rpm.

So the new engine found its way into the 230SL's body and the car became the 250SL. Both models were made

Automatic transmission was standard on the 300D and the car had a top speed of around 90 mph. A turbocharged version was introduced in 1981, with correspondingly higher performance. In a nine-year period over 390,000 300D models, both turbo and standard, were built.

side by side, the 250 ending its run in January 1968 with 5,196 units produced. Then D-B, in its restless pursuit for perfection, enlarged the engine to 169.5 cid (2,778 cc). Installed in the 280S sedan the engine developed 140 hp (DIN) with twin Zenith 35-4-0 INAT carburetors, but was 160 hp with fuel injection in another model, the 280SE. Finally it was rated at 170 hp and in this form it was dropped into the 230/250SL body to become the 280SL.

The air of large American cities was badly polluted, much of it being caused by car exhaust. Los Angeles was particularly affected, its atmosphere on some days becoming a dirty brown smog. State governments acted with laws cutting emissions, then the Federal government stepped in, created the Environmental Protection Agency and passed tough legislation that was a blow to carmakers. Fortunately they realized their responsibilities and endeavored to solve the problem. But emission controls hurt performance across the board including the Mercedes 280SL. In a Europe still dragging its feet on environmental issues, performance of the 280SL was considerably better than the 250. Due to the emission controls the 280SL's performance in America was actually lower than the 230SL, which was unhampered by the controls.

The 280SL was the last of the line, its production ending in March 1971 with a total of 23,885 units built and, between the 230, 250 and 280, almost 49,000 of the luxury sports-tourers having been produced. As well as being the last of the line, even more significantly the 280SL was the last of that six-cylinder engine which D-B began phasing out in 1969 to replace with a similar-powered four-cylinder block. This, however, did not find its way into the next of the Mercedes sports-tourers. A V-8 was to be the power for a new generation of sporty cars

SPECIFICATION
1979 TYPE 450SLC

Engine: V8 K-Jetronic fuel injection. Bore and stroke: 92 x 85mm. 4520cc. Bhp: 218 (DIN) at 5000rpm. Compression ratio: 8.8:1. Manufacturing designation: W107. Built: February/July 1972 – October 1980. Number manufactured: 31,739.

CHAPTER THREE
THE S SERIES AND BEYOND

There was the Model 200, the 200D, the 230 and the 230S; then the 250S and the 250SE, followed by the 280S, 280SE and 280SEL. And thrown in for good measure, the 200D. All these models were part of D-B's enormous fleet of Mercedes, many of which have been described in previous chapters, priced from a shade over $4,000 to well over $20,000 in 1965.

The 200 replaced the 190c sedan in 1965 and it was one of four new models that made their début at the 1965 Frankfurt Auto Show. It used the same four-cylinder engine as the 190 but horsepower had been raised to 95 (DIN). Displacement was 121.27 cubic inches (1,988 cc). Of course, it was the same body that the 190 had used since 1961; the finny Beirut Body. With 70,207 examples built between 1965 and 1968 there is little doubt many found their way to that war-torn Middle Eastern capital of Lebanon.

There was a diesel version as well. Launched at the same time as its gasoline powered brother, the 200D used the 121.27 cubic inch engine which, quite simply, was converted to diesel. A great favorite with taxi-drivers, 161,618 were built in three years, or more than double the gasoline-engined 200.

Produced as the successor to the 220, the 230 and 230S were shown at the 1965 Frankfurt Auto Show. The car was on the same 106.3-inch wheelbase as the 200 series and the 186.5-inch overall length was identical. In these models,

The natural successor to the 280SL was the 350SL, introduced early in 1971. There followed, in quick succession, the 350SLC, 450SL and 450SLC, the latter appearing in 1972. SL versions were two-seaters with a length of 172.4 inches, while the SLC models were stretched to 186.6 inches to accommodate rear seat passengers. The example on these and previous pages is a 1979 450SLC.

SPECIFICATION
1979 TYPE 450SEL

Engine: V8 K-Jetronic fuel injection. Bore and stroke: 92 x 85mm. 4520cc. Bhp: 217 (DIN) at 5000rpm. Compression ratio: 8.8:1. Manufacturing designation: W116. Built: December 1972 – June 1980. Number manufactured: 59,575.

special attention was paid to safety, the front and rear ends designed to yield on impact thus protecting the passengers in the strongly constructed interior. Perhaps this was why these finned Mercedes were so numerous in the war zone of Beirut.

Oddly the 230 was 5 inches shorter than the 220 it replaced; now it was the new 250 series that shared the old 220's wheelbase of 108.3 inches. The 230 used a 139.2 cid (2,281 cc) six while the 250 engine had 152.3 cubic inches (2,496 cc). Horsepower was 130 at 5,400 rpm and the top speed was a creditable 113 mph. What was newsworthy, though, was the car's entirely new body, for the fins were gone, the waistline lowered, and the glass area enlarged. The result was an attractive car in a heavy, purposeful sort of way.

And then there was the 280 – the 280S to be exact. There was also the 280SE and SEL. All shared the same wheelbase as the 250, and the same body with the same overall size. D-B believed in a plethora of models, all on a couple of wheelbases and all sharing two or three body styles in varying degrees of trim. It didn't stop there, for doubtless you will have noticed that each model is part of a series of models; like the 280S for instance.

The Model 280S was a lower middle-priced sedan – or the lowest priced car in the luxury range. Its 169.5-cubic-inch (2,778 cc) engine developed 140 hp (DIN) at 5,200 rpm and the top speed was a reasonable 112 mph. Interestingly, the engine relied on two dual downdraft carburetors rather than the increasingly popular fuel injection system to be found on most other Mercedes models. Both the 280SE and SEL had Bosch's six-plunger fuel injection pump.

Only the 280SE was offered in sedan, coupé and convertible models, the SEL (which went into production in January 1968) being a more luxurious sedan with a 3.9-inch longer wheelbase and 4 inches more in the overall length than the other two. The 280SE hardtop coupé was very similar, if not the same, in design as the 300SE coupé of 1961 to 1967. All these series shared the same suspension, unit body construction and steering and all stayed in production until 1972.

Of the models discussed above, three, the 280 series, were part of D-B's "New Generation" automobiles. All were introduced between 1967 and early 1968 and the majority shared the same body style, coupés and roadsters excepted. Because there were so many different permutations (fifteen New Generation cars alone), it would

Looking very elegant against a background of sea and surf is this timeless 1979 450SEL (these and previous pages) belonging to Mercedes enthusiasts Phyllis and Conrad Mora. Virtually the same car as the 450SE, the SEL has a 4.1-inch longer wheelbase and at 199.2 inches is four inches longer overall. The extra length benefits rear passengers only.

SPECIFICATION
1980 TYPE 300TD

Engine: Five-cylinder. Bore and stroke: 90.9 x 92.4mm. 2998cc. Bhp: 125 (DIN) at 4350rpm. Compression ratio: 21.5:1. Manufacturing designation: S123. Built: 1977 — . Number manufactured: N/A.

take a month of Sundays to describe each individual model.

It has been noted that D-B employed a limited number of wheelbase lengths (the 108.3 inch and 112 inch to mention two) upon which all models are based. The same applies to the engine range. There was a four, a six, an eight and a diesel in use during the late sixties and early seventies. Looking at a list of models one might be led to think each had a different six, for instance; but in fact it was the same engine with varying degrees of power to suit.

The least expensive line of sedans were designated W108 for its unit body/chassis and rode on the 108.3-inch wheelbase. Next came the W109 platform on the 112.2-inch wheelbase. The former carried the 200, 200D (the diesel), the 220 and 220D, all having the gasoline or diesel four-cylinder engine of 121.27 cubic inches. Next came the 230 powered by a six with a 139.9-cubic-inch displacement (2,292 cc). Then the 250, again with a six-cylinder engine displacing 152.4 cubic inches (2,496 cc). Remember, all these cars are New Generation models and not to be confused with the same models mentioned earlier.

The 280 series employed the 108 3 inch wheelbase and it was described a few paragraphs ago. The 280 SEL rode on the 112.2-inch wheelbase and was followed by the 300 SEL which was the top of the line. Both cars used a 169.5 cid (2,778 cc) engine developing 160 hp (DIN).

We return briefly to the 108.3-inch wheelbase to mention a completely new model that was introduced at the end of 1968, the Model 250C/CE, a very attractive coupé based upon the 250 sedan. Its shorter roof was 2 inches lower and the passenger compartment was consequently smaller. Chrome strips on the roof helped the illusion of sportiness. Engine power was the same as the sedan unless the fuel-injected version was ordered, then 150 hp (DIN) was on tap. Four-wheel caliper disc brakes provided superb stopping power thereby enhancing Mercedes' reputation for safety. In some areas such as the U.S. and Britain, the larger 280SE engine was fitted.

Daimler-Benz's powerful and reliable V-8 was being supplied to an increasing number of models. Starting with the 280SE luxury coupé and convertible, the car had a two-year run from 1969 to 1971, only 4,502 units being built. The 3.5-liter engine meant 213.5 cid in American parlance (3,499 cc) and horsepower was 200.

Like the 280SE the 300SEL sedan (on the 112-inch wheelbase) was introduced at the 1969 Frankfurt Auto Show. It was powered by the same 3.5-liter V-8. The car also featured self-leveling and air suspension giving a ride most other luxury cars couldn't match. Then two more V-8 powered 280 models appeared in 1970, the 280SEL and

Previous pages and right: the 300TD diesel station wagon. Introduced at the Frankfurt Auto Show in 1977, the TD uses the six-cylinder diesel engine. Too good to cart farmer's produce to market, this station wagon is more of an up-market family car.

As with most modern cars, the engine bay (above) in the 300TD is crowded. Attractive wheel was standard fare on Mercedes of the early eighties. Interior (facing page bottom) looks almost too luxurious for utilitarian purposes. Wheelbase measures 110 inches and overall length is 186 inches. Top speed is about 90 mph, give or take a mile or two. A turbocharged version went into production in 1980 and the extra boost improved the 300TD's performance.

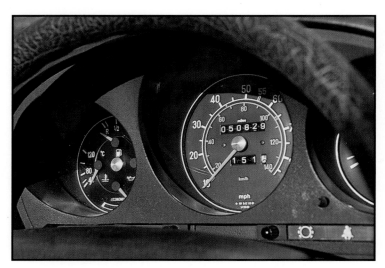

Shown in March 1980, the 380SL roadster (these and previous pages) fitted between the 280 and 500SL models. U.S. versions had a longer stroke to help conform with emissions controls, although this, and the extra weight, cut 14 mph off the top speed – European models topped 134 mph and had better acceleration. Big steering wheel still persists (top), but instruments (above center) are deeply inset to reduce glare.

SPECIFICATION
1982 TYPE 380SL

Engine: V8. Bore and stroke: 88 x 78.9mm. 3839cc. Bhp: 204 (DIN) at 5250rpm. Compression ratio: 8.3:1. Manufacturing designation: W107. Built: 1980 -. Number manufactured: N/A.

the 280SE. Same engine, same power. Both cars lasted only until 1972 before being phased out in readiness for the all-new cars to come.

Looking decidedly heavier, more Teutonic, the 350SL and 350SLC were the 1970 replacements for the 280SL roadsters. Both shared exactly the same V-8 already described. What was quite interesting was that the SL model was a two-seater on a 96.9-inch wheelbase while the SLC had a 111.0-inch wheelbase and was an occasional four-passenger vehicle. The difference in length was quite substantial: 172.8 inches compared to 187 inches, yet the cars looked so alike that it was hard to distinguish one from the other unless they were viewed side by side.

Although quite similar, the body styles of the models sharing the 108.3-inch wheelbase were recognizably different from those using the 112.2-inch. For one thing they were 12 inches shorter and 2 inches narrower, and had a lower grille and less bright trim. Although the new S-class was introduced in 1972, a new 280 series totalling six models came out in 1971, and with the exception of the 280SE and 280SEL, stayed until 1976.

The two that didn't, the 280SE and SEL, were powered by a 2750-cubic-inch (4,520 cc) V-8. This engine was made available for those who wanted more power than the 3.5-liter version would offer. Two wheelbase lengths supported the ultra luxuriant bodies: 108.3 for the SE; 112.2 for the SEL. Both cars sold extremely well during their short life; 13,527 SE models were built; 8,173 SELs were manufactured during the same period from May 1971 until November 1972. Produced at the same time as the latter models was the 300SEL. This sat on the 112-inch wheelbase, had the 4.5-liter V-8 and had more luxury than any equivalent European car. Only 2,553 were built. Emission regulations prevented the 3.5-liter V-8 powered SL and SLC from reaching American shores when the model first appeared. Instead, in an unusual about-face, the U S. was treated to the 4.5-liter 450SL and SLC before Europe – two years before Europe. Americans normally have to wait until Europe has had the car for a year or two.

As sports cars go, the 450SL was a beautiful piece of machinery in terms of handling, roadability and comfort. Emission controls cut its maximum speed to 124 mph; the European version was capable of 134 mph when it was finally introduced in 1973. The "occasional" four-passenger SLC was just as good but was possibly less comfortable for back seat occupants. Before the cars came to the end of the road in 1980, 98,037 of the 450 SL and SLC were built.

One of the world's most beautiful cities was the appropriate place to launch the new Daimler-Benz S-class. Three sedans were unveiled at the 1972 Paris Auto Show: the 280S, the 280SE and the 350SE. The latter had the 3.5-liter M116 V-8 which developed 200 hp (DIN). A carbureted twin-cam six was in the 280S and the 280 SE had the same engine but with fuel injection. This exciting new engine was introduced in 1971 in the new generation 280s described earlier. This DOHC unit had either a Solex downdraft carburetor or electronic fuel injection. The new engine had a much improved combustion chamber and the valves were repositioned for more efficient burning of

115

1981/84 MERCEDES 300CD

A handsome coupé that first appeared in 1977, the diesel-powered 300CD (these and previous pages) is richly appointed in the finest Mercedes tradition. To help give the car more performance, the five-cylinder engine was turbocharged in 1981. This added 45 extra horsepower and took the maximum speed to over 100 mph. As can be seen, the car is a clean design without unnecessary adornment.

SPECIFICATION
1981/84 TYPE 300CD

Engine: Five-cylinder. Bore and stroke: 91 x 92.4mm. 2998cc. Bhp: 125 (DIN) at 4350rpm. Compression ratio: 21.5:1. Manufacturing designation: C123. Built: 1977 – 1981. Number manufactured: 7502.

the noxious exhaust gases. Packaged for the emissions-stringent American market, the engine was considerably detuned over the version sold elsewhere.

Lower, wider and a little longer, the S-class Mercedes was readily identifiable by its traditional grille that had grown longer and wider. Headlights blended smoothly with the front fenders and the wrap-around turn signal lights, dictated by America's outdated lighting laws, cars sold there had to put up with four circular sealed beam units.

One of the areas that needed review was the independent rear suspension system composed of a swing axle. Under certain conditions this suspension was subject to alarming inconsistencies affecting camber. Much midnight oil was burnt at Unterturkheim to correct the problem and resulted in a diagonal-pivot swing axle first tried on the New Generation series. This was actually a semi-trailing arm system with separate half-shafts joined at the differential. Whether equipped with the optional automatic self-leveling struts or not, the new suspension was a marked improvement over the old system.

Bodies, engines and suspension may have changed but wheelbases remained much the same. Cheaper models still used the 108.3-inch, others the 112.6-inch wheelbase. Introduced at the 1973 Frankfurt Auto Show, the 230/4 replaced the 220 and came with a new four-cylinder engine of 140.8 cid and developing 110 hp (DIN). Well over 87,000 were built in its four-year run. A new body with four round headlights came next. For some odd reason the engine lost one horsepower; other than that everything else was little changed on the mechanical side.

As always with D-B there were Mercedes to suit almost every pocket. At the moment we are still hovering around the Seventies; major price increases didn't really begin until the Eighties. One model worth a mention is the 240D, which went into production in January 1976. Its four-cylinder 146.7 cid diesel engine (2,402 cc) produced 65 hp (DIN). A little more than virtual twins, the 200D and 220D had engines of 121.27 cid and 134 cid respectively. In 1979 the 240D, along with other models, had a minor facelift and was offered in a long wheelbase eight passenger limousine. Not so many of these are seen in America where there are limousines a-plenty but in Europe it is quite popular.

A freshly designed six-cylinder engine found its way into the 1976 model 250. Designated the M123 the new engine followed the usual overhead camshaft design, being a 154.1 cid unit (2,525 cc) and developed 129 hp (DIN) at 5,500 rpm. Built for both performance and economy, the engine featured a four-bearing crankshaft with nine counterweights for better balance. The overhead camshaft had a single roller chain drive, hydraulic tensioner and a Solex four barrel. Only one other model, the 250T stationwagon shared this engine

Talking about station-wagons, there were a number of them from the mid-seventies onward. There was the 240TD (the TD means Touristik und Transport Diesel).which was first shown at Frankfurt. Its power unit was the four-cylinder

SPECIFICATION
1985 TYPE 500SEC

Engine: V8. Bosch mechanical with air flow sensor. Bore and stroke: 96.5 x 85mm. 4973cc. Bhp: 230 (DIN) at 4750rpm. Compression ratio: 9.2:1. Manufacturing designation: W126. Built: October 1981 – . Number manufactured: N/A.

diesel (OM616) of 146.4 cid (2,404 cc). Although D-B had been manufacturing cars since 1886 (Daimler and Benz were separate companies then) this was the first station-wagon ever built by the factory, production beginning at D-B's Bremen factory in May 1978.

Sharing the five-cylinder diesel engine with the 300D sedan introduced in 1975, was the 300TD station-wagon. Designated OM617, the diesel was a fresh approach to engine design (Audi came out shortly after with a five-cylinder gasoline engine). It was claimed to be economical and much smoother than four cylinders. Like all D-B engines, OM617 had an overhead camshaft and it featured a six main bearing crank. Automatic transmission was standard. As far as acceleration was concerned, the 300TD was a non-starter – it took 20 seconds to reach 60.

Two other wagons, the 230T and 250T shared the same four- and six-cylinder engines as their respective sedan brothers. The same range of station-wagons is with us to this day, and one, the 300TD, has its five-cylinder diesel engine turbo-charged. In this state a 0 to 60 dash could be accomplished in 16 seconds – not much better, really, but then who needs musclecar performance from a wagon?

The company entered the Eighties in good condition.

Hailed as makers of the best-engineered cars in the world, Daimler-Benz sell almost all it can export to the U.S. Both Cadillac and Lincoln have Mercedes influence in their current designs, and both luxury car divisions worry about Mercedes' steady erosion of their place in American life.

Some very special cars came out of Unterturkheim during the Eighties, cars that stated once and for all that Mercedes-Benz were supreme. Among these were the 380/500SEC coupés. First shown at Frankfurt, the 380 and 500SEC models literally stopped the show. They had sprung from the new S-class series premiered two years earlier and were without doubt the most handsome Mercedes to emerge since the 300SL Gullwing and roadster made their way into the automotive Hall of Fame a quarter of a century earlier.

Low, lithe and possessing a beautifully raked back roof-line, the SEC had a drag coefficient of 0.34. Both employed light alloy V-8 engines, the 380 displacing 234.3 cubic inches (3,839 cc) and rated at 204 hp, while the 500 had a 303 cid (4,973 cc) and developed 231 hp. In the interests of lightness, hood, trunk lid and bulkhead were made of light alloy – important when wishing to be convincing in the quest for fuel economy. Whether or not this was the first

One of the reasons why it will take so long to wrest the title "Best Car in the World" from Mercedes is the superlative 500SEC (these and previous pages). Introduced at the 1981 Frankfurt Show with the identical but smaller-engined 380SEC, the new car took the motoring world by storm.

Quality is but a thin veneer on many luxury cars, but not so with Mercedes. A high standard of finish is found on areas where most people might not think to look, such as the door sides – no sign of spot weld marks here. The interior (above) shouts quality. The 500SEC even has seat belts that offer themselves to driver and passenger once the doors are closed. With a speed of over 140 mph, the rear view (right) is what most of us will see on the highway.

priority, D-B achieved 21.5 mpg out of the 380 and a very good 20.5 from the 500.

In American guise both cars did not have the punch of their European brothers; a U.S. 500 SEC could do 0-60 in about 8 seconds. In Europe that reduced to about 6.5 seconds. There was little difference in top speed, though. The American version had a 140 mph maximum, while the European had about 145. Everything about these cars was of the finest quality in the tradition of first-class travel as it was known before the Second World War. Only the finest materials were used inside and out, and the interior left all but possibly Rolls-Royce, Jaguar and Aston-Martin behind. The most expensive American-made car has an interior equivalent to a Moskvich by comparison. Not only that, these cars have a superb ride with the handling of a thoroughbred. Noisier, perhaps, than a Cadillac or a Rolls, but that can be forgiven for the 380/500 SECs are driver cars, not push-button automatons.

I was fortunate to have a 500 SEC on test for two weeks in 1985, and from the experience of having driven many cars, I can honestly say that I have never driven a better one. The model boasted a full complement of accessories and equipment: air conditioning, four-speed automatic, Blaupunkt AM/FM radio cassette player, leather seating surfaces, ABS brakes, power adjustable seats. What I particularly liked was the arm that automatically proffered the seat belt and wouldn't go away until you had taken it.

For the driver there is no finer car built: its ride and handling are exceptional. Because the model I was driving was the European version, it was incredibly fast, too. The ABS brakes convinced me that every car should be so endowed: from 75 mph the brakes pulled the 500 to a halt in a straight line, every time. Only one car that I know of could possibly out-handle the 500 (now the 560 SEC), and that car is the Corvette ZR-I. But then the ZR-I is an out-and-out sports car. I wonder how it would fare against the new Mercedes 500 SL?

In 1979 Daimler-Benz unveiled the redesigned S-class Mercedes. The new shape took into account the fad for aerodynamic efficiency. Aerodynamics had really taken root in the seventies because it had been shown that good drag coefficients helped economy and performance. One of the first aerodynamic wind-tunnel tested cars was Chrysler's 1934 Airflow; later on, in 1969 and 1970, Chrysler built the wind-cheating Dodge Daytona and Plymouth Superbird, and these cars proved that aerodynamics win races, too.

Because D-B had followed the aerodynamic route, the design of the new models resulted in a drag coefficient improvement of 14 per cent over the preceding S-class bodies. The hood line was lower, the windshield raked back further and there was a definite wedge shape to the cars in profile. Lighter weight materials were used in the construction of all models and the 167.6-cubic-inch DOHC six, used in the least expensive series of luxury sedans, the 280S/SE/SEL models, was improved for better economy and efficiency.

The new 280 and 380 series shared the same 115.5-inch wheelbase and stretched out to 196.6 inches overall. Width

This magnificent 420SEL (previous pages and right) belongs to Georgia television station owners, the Brissettes, and is pictured outside their Boca Raton residence.

SPECIFICATION
1986 TYPE 420SEL

Engine: V8. 5597cc. Bhp:238 (DIN) at 4800rpm. Compression ratio: 9.0:1. Net torque: 287 at 2500.

Powered by the new M116 lightweight 256 cid V8, the 420SEL was the mid-range sedan out of eight S-class models introduced at the 1985 Frankfurt Show. The engine developed 218 bhp at 5,200 rpm and could propel the car to a maximum speed of 135 mph. As can be seen from the understated elegance, this is definitely a car for the rich and famous.

was 71.1 inch, trim when compared to the few wallowing dinosaurs still left panting on America's freeways. A few years on and cars of Mercedes' size would be considered large by most people. Also to become rare were the V-8 engines; fortunately Mercedes didn't join the rush in abandoning theirs when cries for economy were loud and strong. So the 1979 new 380SE/SEL boasted a powerful 233-cubic-inch (3,818 cc) V-8 that whistled the cars up to 134 mph and returned 17.6 mpg (US). (SEL stands for the long wheelbase model.)

Three versions of Mercedes new V-8 were available: two for Europe and one for the U.S. All were constructed of new lightweight materials including silicon/aluminum alloy. In fact the American version displaced 3,839 cc, developed less horsepower and had a top speed at least 19 mph shy of the European model. Most of the specifications mentioned herein, unless otherwise stated, are for European versions. Therefore the 380SEL rode on a 121-inch wheelbase and had an overall length of 202 inches, as did the 280SEL. American specification 380SELs were 208 inches long.

Almost 5 liters (4,973 cc) of light alloy V-8 powered the top-of-the-line 500SE/SEL. Wheelbase was 112.4 inches on the SE and 116.3 on the SEL. Overall lengths were 196.6 and 202.1 inches respectively. With the introduction of the new 5-liter engine the famous 6.9-liter unit was no more. Defending the change, Chief of Development, Werner Breitschwerdt of D-B, said the 5-liter engines were "...equal or even superior to our 450SEL 6.9 in design and equipment".

Whatever the reasons, the new 500SE/SEL models were powerful cruisers with a 140 mph top speed and only 7.5 seconds to 60. The degree of refinement on these and other S-class Mercedes was second to none. The suspension system, consisting of independent front and rear, coil springs, diagonal swing axle anti-roll bars, front and rear and level control was nothing short of the best as any drive would reveal. By the mid-eighties all these Mercedes had ABS braking control. Then the craftsmanlike interiors were equipped with all the extras modern man expects in his carriage.

A new concept in Mercedes motoring arrived in 1982. Strictly-speaking it was an old concept last seen in the days of the 170V: a small Mercedes, the 190 and 190E. At 174 inches long on a 104.9-inch wheelbase, the 190 was quite petite, but its philosophy followed the larger cars, from engineering to style.

Years of testing and evaluating had taken place before the 190 was finally okayed for production. It was a scaled-down version of the S-class W126 chassis and was designated W201. When finally shown to a group of motoring journalists in Spain, the 190 was seen as a head-on competitor to certain BMW models, Audi, Volvo and others of the same power, performance and price. It was also better than most.

The reason for the 190 was stringent new fuel economy legislation from America, Daimler-Benz' most important overseas market. Management knew it would be impossible to meet corporate averages with its existing cars, hence the 190. Market research showed there were many young, affluent customers just waiting to buy a Mercedes ... provided the price was right.

Freshly designed four cylinder ohc engines, both

Fourteen years of refinement and engineering resulted in the last of the popular W107 body style, the 1986 560SL (previous pages and right). Expressly built for the American market to discourage the large-scale importation of European 500SL models that had to be converted to meet American emissions and safety standards, the 560SL would last for five seasons.

Amber turn signals (top) were retained for the U.S. market, but headlamps (above center) are in deference to America's archaic lighting laws. Good looking wheels (above) appear to be a Mercedes trademark if the last thirty years are anything to go by. Photo previous pages and right shows a return to the concave roof. Engine is a 338.5 cid V8 offering a top speed of 137 mph.

gasoline and diesel, were specified. The American market would have a fuel-injected 2.3 gasoline unit compared to the European derivative which would be a 2.0 liter engine using a downdraft carburetor. Horsepower of the 140.3 cubic inch engine was 113 in the U.S. while the 121.72 cid European engine developed 90 (DIN). This is where it becomes awkward. The U.S. measurement is SAE, not DIN. SAE gives the horsepower from an engine block devoid of accessories; DIN, by far the most accurate, takes the developed power from a complete engine ready to install in a car.

The suspension system of the 190 was very refined, and quite different from what had gone before. Gone was the diagonal swing axle; in its place a multi-link arrangement for the rear. Gas-filled shock absorber struts combined with wishbones made up the front suspension and there was anti-dive control at front and rear. Also featured was anti-squat control, coil springs and anti-roll bars.

Since its introduction the 190 series has done particularly well. It is expensive but not excessively so and keeps in line with its nearest rivals. Nine months after its initial introduction D-B launched a real winner. Bedecked in spoilers, skirts and air dams, the car developed 185 hp from its 140.3 cid engine. The U.S. SAE rating was 167 hp, top speed was a staggering 140 plus mph, and it took only 7.3 seconds to reach sixty. In much this guise, the 190E 16v broke three world records at Nardo, Italy, in August 1983. It covered 50,000 kilometers at an average of 154.06 mph, managed 1,000 kilometers at 153.30 mph, and was driven for 24 hours at 153.30 mph. Not bad for a new car with a new engine – that, however, is what makes a Mercedes special!

There is a diesel-engined 190 as well; the 190D has only 72 hp, but can attain 100 mph without difficulty. Remember the clatter a diesel makes when idling? D-B engineers managed to reduce noise levels by half over what went before. Apart from the engine, the 190D is identical to the gasoline car.

In 1984 there came a new 200 model. It was one of seven different models that would share the new W124 body style which replaced the W123, then nine years old. Four of the models were gasoline and three diesel. The 121.9 cid four-cylinder engine powered the 200, while the enlarged (140.3 cid) version took care of the 230 model. As for the 260 and 300, both used six-cylinder engines: in the 260E the displacement was 158.6 cubic inches; in the 300 this was 180.8 (or 2,599 cc and 2,962 cc respectively). Otherwise all the models shared much the same suspension, steering, brakes etc. – it all came out of the same parts-bin, anyway. All three diesel versions used different engines. The 200D came with four cylinders and was a diesel clone of the 121.9-cubic-inch gasoline unit. Not so with the 250D. This had a newly developed five-cylinder diesel engine developing 90 hp and displacing 152.4 cubic inches (2,497 cc). As for the 300D, this had a six-cylinder diesel of 182.8 cid and 109 horsepower. Top speed was a useful 118 mph, but 13.7 seconds to 60 was still a bit sluggish.

Which brings us up to date.

Never resting, always improving, Daimler-Benz reached

Mindful of the need to conserve energy, Mercedes embarked upon a down-sizing program which resulted in the 190 series first shown in late 1982. The model shown on these and previous pages is the 190D powered by a four-cylinder ohc diesel unit (MO 601) displacing 121.71 cu. in. First shown at Frankfurt in 1983, the 190D could deliver 35 mpg.

Top: excellence, reliability, luxury ... these are just some of the qualities the distinctive Mercedes emblem brings to mind. The interior of the 190 (above) is almost as spacious as that of full-size sedans, while the sloped back grille and steeply raked windshield help aerodynamic efficiency with a coefficient of 0.33.

SPECIFICATION 1987 TYPE 190E

Engine: Four-cylinder. Bore and stroke: 95,5 x 80.25mm. 2299cc. Bhp: 185 (DIN) at 6200rpm. Compression ratio: 10.5:1. Manufacturing designation: W201. Built 1983 -. Number manufactured: N/A.

To further enhance the 190's growing reputation, Mercedes introduced the 190E 2.3 16-valve high performance model (these and previous pages) at the 1983 Frankfurt Auto Show. Developed by Cosworth engineers, its 2.3-liter (140.3 cid) engine had four valves per cylinder, a light alloy cylinder head with twin overhead camshafts, and Bosch LE Jetronic fuel injection. Very fast, the car is capable of a top speed of over 145 mph. Top: the 190's interior is plush as well as practical, and no doubt the rear spoiler (above) really serves a purpose, too.

its 100th anniversary in 1986 and celebrated with the 560SEC and 560SEL sedan. Length was 199.2 and 208 inches respectively. Power came from the 5.6-liter V-8 in abundance; by now it was 238 hp. The SEL exuded extravagance, and this was matched by its price of $58,900. Within the high-bracket price range of automobiles, however, it was still a bargain when compared with the likes of a Rolls or Ferrari Testa Rossa. The 560 SEC, however, much as I like it, was in my opinion overpriced.

Two new 190 sedans were introduced in 1987. One was the 190E 2.6, the first 190 model to come equipped with a six-cylinder engine – the same unit that powered the 1987 260/300 range. The other added a turbo-charger to its diesel engine, thus adding 30 extra horses to the 190D 2.5 Turbo.

For 1988 the 190 series undertook a pruning operation for the American market after finding its sales had fallen. Two years before, the 190 was Mercedes' most popular car in North America. By 1987 this had changed to the mid-size 260/300 range. Two models disappeared; the 190E 2.3 16 valve, the five-cylinder diesel turbo-charged 190D because of durability problems. Safe was the 2.6-liter six 190E and the normal 2.5 diesel took over from the troublesome one. This was D-B's only diesel engine on American shores for 1988. Finally, the 2.3-liter four-cylinder 190E returned at the colossal price of $28,450. Which was nothing compared to the 1987 2.3-liter 16-valve. That was $43,320!

The year 1989 marked a momentous event in motor racing; the return of Mercedes to competition. Le Mans was the venue; the same venue Mercedes withdrew from, after one of its cars somersaulted into the crowd killing 80 spectators 34 years earlier. The Silver Arrows were back!

The drivers had been Jochen Mass, Manuel Reuter and Stanley Dickens. Then there were Mauro Baldi, Kenny Acheson and Gianfranco Brancatelli. The final car had Jean-Louis Schlesser, Jean-Pierre Jabouille and Alain Cudini – men who would create anew, the legend of Mercedes-Benz.

Peter Saubers was one of the reasons D-B came back into racing He was racing Mercedes-powered cars at Le Mans from 1985 until 1987 with half-hearted support from the factory. In 1988 D-B decided to announce its return to racing. A team of Silver Arrows came to Le Mans but withdrew when, during practice, one of the team cars

blew a tire at high speed. Memories of 1955 die hard with Mercedes. But D-B came back in 1989, with Peter Saubers fielding a team of Silver Arrow C9s powered by new M199 four-valve V-8 engines...that's four valves per cylinder.

Mercedes won. Saubers team came home first and second. It might have been a clean sweep had not the fourth placed Mercedes suffered engine problems; gearboxes proved a weak link. Problems arose because the engines produced more power than the boxes could handle. Nevertheless, it was that power, coupled with reliability, that brought success. The average speed of the winning Mass/Reuter/Dickens car was 136.613 mph. Many had wished for a long time to see Mercedes racing again and here they were, after a 34-year absence proving themselves mightier than ever and a force to be reckoned with on the race-tracks of the world.

For 1989, a passenger air bag was optional on all Mercedes S-cars . Ahead of the rest once again, Mercedes have had driver's air bags as standard since 1986. Apart from the air bags there was nothing new. Six S-class models were offered in America, these being the 300SE, 300SEL, 420SEL, 560SEL. 560SEC and 560SL, All were penalized in America for failing to meet the government's Corporate

These and previous pages: a very rare 1987 300SDL powered by a turbocharged six-cylinder ohc diesel engine. The standard 300SD was equipped with a five-cylinder turbocharged engine. The SDL was, at 208.1 inches, 5.5 inches longer than the SD, and sat on a 5.5 inch-longer wheelbase measuring 121.1 inches. The model first became available in the U.S. in 1986, but disappeared soon afterwards.

Average Fuel Economy, or CAFE for short. The penalty is a Gas Guzzler tax which means each model that fails to pass the CAFE test has to pay a tax on every car sold. In the 300SE's case this would be $650 but a $1500 fine is laid at the door of every 560 SEL that finds a home.

For the second year running D-B trimmed its 190 line still further. All that was left was the 158 horsepower 2.6-liter six-cylinder 190E and Mercedes' only diesel offered in the U.S., the five cylinder 2.5-liter 190D. D-B lowered the 190E's base price late in 1988 by $2,000. The price for this beautifully engineered, well-finished car is $31,590. Faithful as ever and still America's most popular Mercedes, the 260/300 series offered passenger airbags. Models sold in America include the 300TE station-wagon and 300CE coupé. Mechanically the 260 uses the same 2.6-liter unit as that employed by the 2.6 190, but the 300 has a 3-liter version of the same engine. As for the 560SL roadster, this was getting a little long in the tooth even though it was still a car of king's. D-B already knew that and rectified the situation in 1990 with a vision on wheels: the new 500SL

Those who have driven the new 500SL say it is a work of art. One writer in *Autoweek* magazine likened the car to a dancer that Mercedes "made it respond to a beat, react to a rhythm...." Looking over its specifications, at its technology, the 500SL is everything the Cadillac Allante wanted to be, but isn't.

Two models are available in the U.S., another in Europe and the rest of the world. There is the 300SL which has for an engine, a 24-valve, 228-hp dohc six. This 181 cubic inch unit has a cast-iron block and alloy cylinder head. Standard transmission is a five-speed manual. Unlike most cars in which the fifth gear is an overdrive, D-B made its fifth a direct gear. Combined with the right axle ratio (which,

naturally the car has) the fifth direct gear will fulfill economy goals while still satisfying performance buffs. Oh, the automatic transmission also offered has a fifth gear, but this is overdrive only. If prospective buyers are excited

about a fifth gear then they will have to settle for the 300SL as the 500SL is equipped with only the automatic. Dr. Wolfgang Peter, Mercedes chief engineer, says the current manual five-speed box would not be able to handle the torque of the powerful V-8. No doubt this will change if there is enough clamor for a manual compatible with the V-8.

The V-8 engine in the 500SL is a 32-valve! 5.0-liter, 303 cid unit that develops 322 hp! It has an alloy block and heads. Top speed is about 160 mph. Like all Mercedes, the 300 and 500SLs are heavy; 3,975 and 4,163 lbs respectively. Why so heavy? Because D-B subscribes to the logical theory that weight adds strength to car bodies and helps save lives. For years Daimler-Benz has committed itself to building safer than safe cars: the company is very serious about it. And as Mercedes cars are the safest in the world, it bears out their makers' claim.

Part of Mercedes' safety concerns can be found in the new SLs. The seat frames are made of die-cast magnesium and are very strong. In the event of a side impact the frames will form a crush-resistant buffer zone for the occupant by deforming slowly, thus absorbing most of the energy out of the impact. Another feature is an automatic roll-bar, which can be raised by the driver or it will rise instantly and automatically in the event of a roll-over.

Other visible safety features are seat-backs that lock automatically once the car is moving, and seat-belts are built into the seats and provide, according to those who have tried them, the most comfortable and secure harness

If the futuristic 1990 500SL roadster (these and previous pages) is anything to go by, this is the shape of things to come. A work of automotive art, it replaced the 560SL, whose body had been refined as far as it would go. The 500SL is a true state-of-the-art automobile; possibly the nearest thing to perfection on wheels that one can find.

Previous pages: a once great American institution, the drive-in theatre is virtually no more – a victim of television and teenagers with no imagination. But a great German institution, the Mercedes Benz, will be around as long as there is gasoline ... and probably longer. The 420 SEL's 4.2-liter fuel injected V8 whisks the car along in silence and style. Equipped with power telescopic steering, power seats with memory, automatic climate control, the 420SEL has all the features one could reasonably hope for in an automobile.

to be found in a car.

The seats have a ten-way power adjustment and three-position memory, a standard removable aluminum hardtop, leather or cloth seats, all the necessary power gimmicks and handsome lines that will still be fresh at the close of the century. Suspension is much the same as before: struts, gas shocks, wishbones, multilink rear anti-sway bars, etc. However, this car is expensive, very expensive: between $69,000 and $73,000, depending on the model.

Most of the rest of Mercedes' 1990 fleet is relatively unchanged. One interesting innovation for 1990 is the computer-controlled four-wheel drive system. This has been available in Europe for two years or more and will be offered on the 300E sedan and 300TE station-wagon. When the car takes off, the four-wheel drive system automatically engages to provide greater traction. Once under way, the car automatically changes to rear-wheel drive only; sensors determine when conditions suit fwd and then transfer some of the engine torque to the front wheels.

With the advent of the aggressive Japanese Lexus and Infiniti luxury cars, Mercedes has a tougher battle ahead to keep on top. Reports from Germany talk of an amazing new S-class sports sedan, and sneaked photographs reveal a beautifully shaped car that looks as though it means business. A V-12 engine is planned for the new S-class when it goes on sale in 1992, which should be a very interesting year because we are promised great things from GM, and there may well be a new Jaguar.

Somehow I do not think these reports will ruffle Mercedes unduly. Slowly but surely Mercedes-Benz automobiles have marched to the summit, to be recognized as the very best cars in the world.

159